THE GLORIOUS YEARS

OF THE

LMS

LONDON MIDLAND & SCOTTISH RAILWAY

PETER TUFFREY

GREAT NORTHERN

ACKNOWLEDGEMENTS

I would like to thank the following people for their help: Roger Arnold, David Burrill, John Chalcraft, Paul Chancellor, Peter Crangle, John Law, Hugh Parkin, Andrew Warnes.

Special thanks are due to my son Tristram Tuffrey for his help and encouragement throughout the course of this project.

Unless otherwise stated, all photographs from the author's collection.

In the latter years of the LMS, colour photography had only just begun and was an expensive activity that very few photographers could afford. Consequently, less than 70 colour photographs of LMS subjects are known to have survived, and the quality of these in many cases is poor. The Author would like to express sincere thanks to David P. Williams for his skill in producing the fine colour illustrations which adorn the covers of this book. They have been painstakingly put together by digitally adding colour to original monochrome photographs, with the aim of re-creating what the photographer could see in the camera viewfinder when the shutter was released.

Great Northern Books Limited
PO Box 1380, Bradford, BD5 5FB
www.greatnorthernbooks.co.uk

© Peter Tuffrey 2023

ISBN: 978-1-914227-55-4

Design and layout: David Burrill

CIP Data
A catalogue for this book is available from the British Library

INTRODUCTION

One hundred years have passed from the formation of the largest British railway company – the London Midland & Scottish Railway. This was also the biggest transport concern in the world. Following some initial problems, the LMSR was able to focus on serving passengers and customers to a high standard up to the Second World War. During the conflict, the LMSR made a valuable contribution to the war effort in terms of motive power provision, movement of goods and war materials.

The Grouping of the railways was the result of the First World War. At the start of hostilities, the British rail system was taken over by the Government under the Railway Executive Committee to consolidate operations. The success that was achieved through this brought up questions about making the arrangement permanent. Nationalisation of the railway system had been discussed as early as the 1840s and questions were asked as to the morality of a number of enterprises. At the end of the First World War a select committee was formed to gather data and make recommendations for the future. Sir Eric Geddes of the North Eastern Railway was given this job and reported there were several levels of mergers that could take place whilst advising against returning to original arrangements. In 1919, Geddes was made Minister of Transport and he presented his white paper in the following year suggesting regional groups of railways. He was against Nationalisation as being an unwieldy enterprise with lack of accountability and likely source of financial waste. He was informed on the latter by his position as Chairman of the Committee on National Expenditure which looked at ways to reduce Government spending in the post-war financial climate. Geddes recommended cutting nearly £90,000,000 from the budget, though just over £50,000,000 was finally approved. This was also likely a reason against Nationalisation of the railways at the time.

There was much opposition to the proposals from the railway companies but negotiations eventually allowed the passage of the Railways Act 1921. The idea of splitting into regions was modified to larger areas organised along the course of the main lines. The London Midland & Scottish Railway was formed from several large concerns, as well as a number of smaller routes and joint operations. The two main constituents were the London & North Western Railway, which had absorbed the Lancashire & Yorkshire in early 1922 to boost the route mileage to approx. 2,700, and Midland Railway, with the latter having over 2,000 miles of rail lines. Supporting were the Caledonian Railway (1,000 miles), Glasgow & South Western Railway and Highland Railway (500 miles), North Staffordshire Railway and Furness Railway (220 and 250 miles respectively). The LMSR had holdings in the Midland & Great Northern Joint Railway, Somerset & Dorset Joint Railway and the Cheshire Lines Committee. The Railways Act 1921 was approved in August 1921 and was set to take effect on 1st January 1923.

With the LNWR being the largest company, the assumption would be the most influence was placed with the group in the LMSR. Yet, three of the top officers had been lost within the previous ten years, allowing the men with seniority in the Midland Railway to take the influential roles within just a few years after amalgamation. Sir Guy Granet became Chairman in 1924 whilst J.H. Follows was Chief General Superintendent and Sir Henry Fowler took the Chief Mechanical Engineer's role in 1925. With these and several others, the LMSR took on a Midland Railway bias which antagonised the former employees of the LNWR. The bureaucracy feared by Geddes as a result of Nationalisation was also present in the smaller, yet still vast LMSR company. For example, goods agents on smaller lines had to refer to regional centres for authorisation on deals which often took time. Developing relations with customers over a number of years, these goods agents were likely left adrift by people who had no idea of local conditions.

The outward signs of the Midland influence for the general public were subtle at first as the company's Crimson Lake was adopted for standard passenger livery for locomotives. The policy of using two locomotives on modestly loaded trains was also favoured and spread on to the West Coast Main Line where the practice was not suited owing to the long distances involved. The first new locomotive designed under the LMSR was the Hughes 'Crab' Class 2-6-0 for mixed traffic duties and this managed to escape complete 'Midlandisation', being closer to Lancashire & Yorkshire practice. The change in policy was seen when Fowler took office as a large number of MR-influenced 2P and 4P 4-4-0s were built, in addition to 4F 0-6-0s, 3F 0-6-0Ts and 2-6-4T/2-6-2Ts for intermediate passenger duties. A slight exception was the 'Royal Scot' Class which was the result of pressure from the running department for a powerful express engine following experience with a Collett 'Castle' Class 4-6-0 loaned from the Great Western Railway. Fowler's Royal Scots were on hand for the improvement in main line passenger timings in 1928 when the long-standing Anglo-Scottish limits were broken.

After an indifferent start to the company's life, the 1930s saw a change of outlook for the LMSR despite a tough economic background. Firstly, Sir Guy Granet made way for Sir Josiah Stamp and a company reorganisation took place. Then, Fowler retired and William Stanier was recruited from the Great Western Railway. He was set the task of modernising the rolling stock and despite some initial teething troubles this was achieved through the introduction of several important classes. He first addressed the low numbers of suitable express passenger engines with the 'Princess Royal' Pacifics which appeared in 1933. These were followed by the 5XP 'Jubilee' Class 4-6-0 that were to play a supporting role on other express and intermediate duties. Whilst these had three cylinders, Stanier also produced a two-cylinder version for passenger and freight, the Class 5 which went on to be the most numerous LMSR locomotive as over 700 were built to 1948, with more appearing up to 1951 when 842 were in service. A similar number of his heavy freight locomotives, the 8F Class, appeared, though many of these were built under Government orders during the Second World War to help with the movement of war materials. Some were loaned to the other 'Big Four' railway companies and taken into stock by the LMSR in the post-war period.

Stanier's most prestigious class was the 'Coronation' Pacific and this was built for a new train introduced between Euston and Glasgow. This had an improved timing to six hours thirty minutes and was named the 'Coronation Scot' to celebrate the accession of George VI. An improved train was arranged and a new set was planned before the war halted the project. The new locomotive was an improved version of the earlier 'Princess Royal' Class with larger boiler and firebox, increased diameter driving wheels, bigger piston valves and better motion arrangement. A request from the marketing department complicated the design process. The London & North Eastern Railway introduced a similar service in 1937 using their streamlined Gresley A4 Class Pacific developed in 1935. The streamlining had generated much publicity, as was the case with similar locomotives in Europe and America. Some of these were designed using wind tunnels whereas others were built to exploit some of the interest generated by the unusual shapes.

Stanier and his design team agreed to the appeal and turned to the wind tunnel to determine a suitable shape. Luckily, this fit within loading gauge limits which were tight owing to the 'Coronation' locomotive's large size. Five were erected initially and had a special livery of blue with silver lining running rearward from the nose of the engine, along the carriages to the rear of the set. On a demonstration journey from Euston to Crewe no. 6220 *Coronation* achieved 114 mph which became the British steam speed record for a time. Later, just before the war, another 'Coronation' Pacific achieved a British horsepower record. With 20 carriages and the Dynamometer car (610 tons), the locomotive had a drawbar horsepower reading of over 2,500 at one point and this beat the LNER's P2 no. 2001 *Cock o' the North*'s 2,100 from earlier in the decade.

In 1933, Fowler's 'Royal Scot' Class 4-6-0 no. 6100 *Royal Scot* was shipped to America and toured the country before becoming an exhibit at the Chicago Century of Progress event. At the end of the 1930s, the World's Fair exhibition was held in New York and no. 6220 was chosen to represent the LMSR along with the 'Coronation Scot' train formation. The party left England in early 1939 and due to return at the end of the year but was held up by the outbreak of war. Both trips were successful for the LMSR and helped to increase the awareness of the company with the American public.

The late 1930s saw plans formulated to deal with conflict in Europe. The Railway Executive Committee convened again to plan how to move men, war materials and essential supplies. When war was declared, the LMSR fell under the control of the REC and one of the first tasks was the evacuation of children from urban areas, with nearly 1,500 trains used. Then, around 200 trains transported troops bound for Scandinavia and 44 sets of carriages were sent to help with the Dunkirk evacuation. At the end of the war, nearly 90,000 special passenger trains had run on LMSR metals. Just over 49,000 war-related goods trains were scheduled, along with 27,000 for petrol tankers, 11,000 for ammunition and 2,600 conveyed mails related to the armed forces. The LMSR had one of the largest engineering departments in the world with several main workshops and dozens of subsidiary factories employing nearly 25,000 people. These establishments were quick to assist with the war effort and an additional 5,000 employees were necessary to keep up with the work. This ranged from small items – searchlight projectors, rifle components, bent rails for roadblocks, etc. – to heavy equipment such as tanks – Centaurs, Covenanters and Matildas. The shops also contributed many aircraft parts for Horsa gliders, Hurricanes and Typhoons as well as Hampden and Lancaster bombers. In order to reduce the need for new materials, parts were reclaimed from damaged craft.

Towards the end of the war, Sir William Stanier retired and was briefly replaced by Charles Fairburn, who died in 1945. The last CME of the LMSR was H.G. Ivatt and he produced three designs: Class 2 2-6-0 and 2-6-2T; 4MT 2-6-0. These were built to meet the needs of the post-war world where ease of maintenance and servicing was a priority.

Whereas there was an uncertainty of the direction of Britain's railways following the First World War, the election of a Labour Government in 1945 signalled the inevitability of Nationalisation, which was a key policy for the party. The railway companies perhaps welcomed this, as the war had taken a huge toll on rolling stock and infrastructure. A massive amount of capital was necessary for the reconstruction and rehabilitation of the railways. With the financial position of three of the 'Big Four' strained pre-war, the task was likely beyond a private concern. The Transport Act 1947 created the British Transport Commission and British Railways which split the 'Big Four' into several regions as Geddes had envisaged 30 years earlier. When the LMSR ceased to exist on 1st January 1948, the territory became the London Midland Region and Scottish Region.

The LMSR existed for just 25 years and during that time the company, the officers and employees were able to create a lasting legacy of hard work, achievement and innovation. *The Glorious Years of the LMS* celebrates this period with over 250 evocative images of the company's locomotives, carriages, road vehicles and stations. Though the number of people who can remember the LMSR first-hand is diminishing, the company's locomotives are well-represented in preservation with over 70 saved from the scrapyard. Hopefully, these and the images in this book will continue to inspire interest in the LMSR, steam traction and British railway history for years to come.

Peter Tuffrey
Doncaster, May 2023

CONTENTS

LOCOMOTIVES   6

Express Passenger 6
Diesel 48
Passenger Tender Locomotives 49
Passenger Tanks 62
Railmotor 74
Mixed Traffic 74
Freight 81
Garratt 88
Tanks 91

CARRIAGES   94

WAR WORK   125

ROAD VEHICLES   128

RAILWAY STATIONS   154

LOCOMOTIVES
EXPRESS PASSENGER
ROYAL SCOT

Above NO. 6100
As a publicity exercise, the London Midland & Scottish Railway sent no. 6100 *Royal Scot* to America in 1933. At the start of the year, the locomotive spent two months in works being prepared for the journey and is in the middle of this process here. Note the smokebox nameplate and bracket for a searchlight later fitted at the top of the door.

Opposite above NO. 6100
No. 6100 *Royal Scot* was ready for the summer season of 1927. Constructed by the North British Locomotive Company, the cab has been pictured when new.

Opposite below NO. 6101 – CAMDEN SHED
On April 23rd 1939, no. 6101 *Royal Scots Grey* takes water at Camden shed. The tender is a Stanier 4,000-gallon example from a Jubilee Class 4-6-0. The Royal Scots were given priority in an exchange that occurred in the mid-1930s. Photograph by John P. Wilson from Rail Archive Stephenson courtesy Rail-Online.

Above NO. 6106 – CAMDEN

No. 6106 *Gordon Highlander* was completed at the NBLC's Queen's Park Works in September 1927. The two workshops had different works plates and the diamond-shaped Queen's Park plate is visible above on the side of the smokebox. The engine's first permanent allocation was Camden and is in the area here. For much of the 1930s, no. 6106 was at Polmadie depot, Glasgow.

Opposite above NO. 6103 – RUGBY STATION

The North British Locomotive Company was contracted to build the first 50 Royal Scot Class 4-6-0s. Twenty-five of these were the product of the company's Queen's Park Works, whilst the others appeared from Hyde Park Works. No. 6103 *Royal Scots Fusilier* was built at the first mentioned in September 1927. Initially without smoke deflectors and unnamed, *Royal Scots Fusilier* was on the locomotive after six months in traffic. The deflectors started to be fitted to the class from 1935. No. 6103 was altered between then and when pictured at Rugby with an express on 15th May 1937. With mineral wagons on the right is Johnson 2F Class 0-6-0 no. 3009. Photograph by Les Hanson from the David Hanson Archive courtesy Rail-Online.

Opposite below NO. 6103

A weak point of the original Royal Scot design was the smokebox. Despite the start of the Second World War, plans were set in motion during 1942 to rebuild a number of the class. Stanier had developed the Type 2A boiler with two Jubilee Class 4-6-0s and this was deemed suitable to crossover the classes. The Royal Scots also received new cylinders which meant overall the engine was lighter and finally allowed the class on to the ex-Midland Main Line. The first locomotive to be transformed was no. 6103 *Royal Scots Fusilier* in June 1943 and another eight were treated to the end of the year. The process was mainly completed by 1950, but 12 remained in original condition and were dealt with up to 1955. No. 6103 had just been rebuilt here and also of note is the double chimney.

Above NO. 6115 – EUXTON

Just south of Preston at Euxton, no. 6115 *Scots Guardsman* has an express for Birmingham during the 1930s. The train had originated in Glasgow and no. 6115 has a '27A' shed code on the smokebox door for Polmadie depot. The engine was there from 1932 to 1939.

Below NO. 6134

Many locomotives were painted black during the Second World War. From 1946 a new variation on this was introduced featuring lining along the running plate, front and rear of the boiler barrel, etc. The font of the number and company branding also changed. No. 6134 *The Cheshire Regiment* models the livery in this image.

Above NO. 6112

Water from an unidentified set of troughs is collected by no. 6112 *Sherwood Forester*'s tender. The locomotive was probably photographed when nearly new as the number is on the tender and LMSR crest on the cab side. Smoke deflector plates were fitted around 1932 and the tender was upgraded in the middle of the decade.

Below NO. 6129 – WILLESDEN JUNCTION STATION

Around 1930, no. 6129 *Comet* has made a stop with an express at Willesden Junction (low level) station. The engine was later renamed *The Scottish Horse* in December 1935. Photograph by J.N. Hall from Rail Archive Stephenson courtesy Rail-Online.

Above NO. 6138 – CAMDEN

Where the West Coast Main Line curved southward to Euston, a locomotive shed was established by the London & Birmingham Railway and was progressively improved over the years. Camden depot was primarily for express engines and Royal Scot no. 6138 *Fury* is there for servicing around 1930. Just to the north of the shed, the LNWR opened a station which connected to the North London Railway and the Chalk Farm station nameboard for this can be glimpsed in the background.

Below NO. 6170

When no. 6399 *Fury*'s high-pressure boiler was deemed a failure, Stanier rebuilt the locomotive with a new boiler similar to that used with his new Jubilee Class. Yet, this also had issues and further development was necessary before successful operation was achieved and the Type 2 boiler fitted was the basis of the Type 2A later used for the Royal Scot rebuilds. No. 6399 was renumbered 6170 in 1935 and renamed *British Legion*.

Above **NO. 6144**

The original naming policy for the Royal Scot Class saw regiment names mixed with those of old, historical locomotives. No. 6144 was initially *Ostrich* before all took military names, then the engine became *Honourable Artillery Company* from January 1933.

Below **NO. 6147 – BRITANNIA BRIDGE**

Crossing from Anglesey to North Wales, no. 6147 *Courier* has an express for Euston in 1933. The engine was later renamed *The Northamptonshire Regiment*. Photograph courtesy Rail Photoprints.

Above NO. 6100

An unprecedented event was the journey of no. 6100 *Royal Scot* to America in 1933. The locomotive acted as an ambassador for the LMSR across 80 cities and travelled over 11,000 miles between 1st May and 11th November. Part of this period was spent at the Century of Progress exhibition in Chicago. Over 3 million people saw the locomotive and the Royal Scot train which was also sent for display. No. 6100 acquired a spotlight and bell for the trip, whilst a cowcatcher also appeared on the buffer beam. All were later removed, though a plate detailing the trip was later fitted below the nameplate. No. 6100 was back in England before Christmas.

Opposite above NO. 6100

After being specially prepared for the American journey, no. 6100 had to be disassembled before transportation across the Atlantic on the SS *Beaverdale*. The chassis is being lifted on to the ship here at Tilbury Dock, with the boiler waiting below.

Opposite below NO. 6100

Some of the crew which travelled with no. 6100 *Royal Scot* pose in front of the locomotive in Chicago. On the left is Fireman J. Jackson, Driver W. Gilbertson is centre and on the right is W.G. Woods, Fitter. A second Fireman, T. Blackett is not in the group.

Above NO. 6399

A 'fad' to develop high-pressure boilers for locomotives gripped Europe in the 1920s. Examples were built in France and Germany, whilst in England Sir Nigel Gresley of the London & North Eastern Railway built W1 Class no. 10000 during 1929. Not to be left out, Fowler obtained authorisation in 1928 for a Royal Scot chassis to be fitted with a Schmidt-Henschel boiler. This type had sections working at different pressures and fed three compound cylinders. The top working pressure was particularly high at 1,400 lb per sq. in. The NBLC was contracted to construct no. 6399 *Fury* and the locomotive appeared in early February 1930, being seen outside the shops above in works grey livery. Sadly, a short time afterwards while on test a tube exploded and killed Mr Lewis Schofield of the Superheater Company, which was acting as an advisor to the LMSR on the project. The locomotive was repaired and tested but did not achieve satisfactory operation. Stanier later rebuilt no. 6399 as no. 6170 *British Legion* with a Type 2 boiler in 1935.

PATRIOT

Above **NO. 5500**

The first Patriot Class 4-6-0 was no. 5500 *Patriot*, but the engine was a rebuilt Claughton Class locomotive, no. 5971 *Croxteth*. No. 5500 was renumbered in 1934 and renamed 1937.

Below **NO. 5502 – HILLMORTON, RUGBY**

An express is with Patriot Class no. 5502 *Royal Naval Division* at Hillmorton, just south of Rugby station, on 21st May 1939. The engine was built in July 1932 and named during 1937. Photograph courtesy Rail-Online.

NO. 5505 – WHITMORE

South of Crewe at Whitmore, Patriot Class no.5505 (named *The Royal Army Ordnance Corps* in 1947) pilots Royal Scot no.6110 *Grenadier Guardsman* with a 'Lakes Express' train in 1938. Photograph from Rail Archive Stephenson courtesy Rail-Online.

Above **NO. 5504**

From the first two Claughton rebuilds, a gap of around 18 months passed before the nominal rebuilds began. No. 5504 was the last of three to be completed at Crewe during July 1932. The locomotive was later named *Royal Signals* in 1937 and has the plate visible in this image from the period.

Below **NO. 5510 – SHEFFIELD MIDLAND STATION**

Patriot Class no. 5510 has an express at Sheffield Midland station during the 1930s. Built at Crewe in August 1932, the engine ran for the next 30 years nameless – one of twelve to do so.

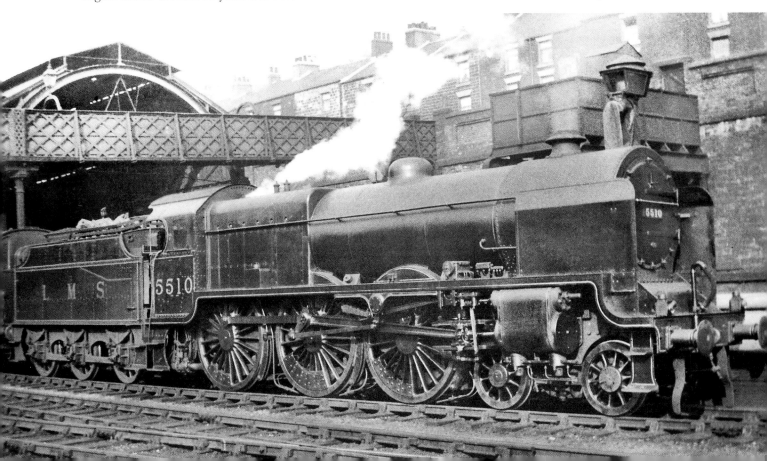

Above **NO. 5517 – NUNEATON**

The introduction of the Royal Scot Class meant the demise of the ex-London & North Western Railway's Claughton 4-6-0. These four-cylinder engines underperformed over the years and the opportunity was taken to rebuild many class members in the early 1930s. Whilst several parts from the original engines were reused on the first two conversions, remaining examples saw fewer components carried over. A total of 52 were erected by Crewe and Derby Works between 1930 and 1934. No. 5517 appeared from Crewe Works in February 1933 and remained unnamed. The locomotive was condemned in June 1962. No. 5517 has an express at Nuneaton. Photograph courtesy Rail-Online.

Below NO. 5512 –
NOTTINGHAM MIDLAND STATION

The Midland Counties Railway opened the first station at Nottingham in 1839 with the line to Derby. Just under a decade later, the site moved to one a short distance away and this continues to serve rail passengers. The buildings have changed as the station was rebuilt comprehensively in the early 20th century. This was designed by locally-based architect A.E. Lambert, who also designed the Great Central Railway's Nottingham Victoria, the line from which incredibly crosses Nottingham Midland on the bridge in the top left. No. 5512 *Bunsen* has a southbound express on 29th June 1939. Photograph by John P. Wilson from Rail Archive Stephenson courtesy Rail-Online.

NO. 5525 – EUSTON STATION

Though carrying two names in the 1930s, no. 5525 appears to be unnamed in this image. The locomotive is seen arriving at Euston with an FA Cup special in 1938. When rebuilt at Derby in March 1933, *E. Tootal Broadhurst* was carried, then in the later 1930s *Colwyn Bay* was used. Photograph by C.R.L. Coles from Rail Archive Stephenson courtesy Rail-Online.

Above NO. 5530 – EUSTON STATION

A particularly well-presented Patriot is at Euston station in 1938. No. 5530 was recently named *Sir Frank Ree*, after the General Manager of the LNWR, taking the title from original rebuild no. 5501 (5902) which became *St. Dunstans*. Photograph by C.R.L. Coles from Rail Archive Stephenson courtesy Rail-Online.

Below NO. 5538

In the late 1930s, no. 5538 *Giggleswick* poses for the camera in a fresh coat of Crimson Lake livery with Derby Scroll-style numbers and lettering.

Above NO. 5538 – SETTLE STATION

Brigadier General Sir Harold Hartley, Vice-President of the LMSR, was invited to the Speech Day at Giggleswick school on 2nd July 1938. At the close of his own speech, he said: 'The LMS Railway Co. [are] justly proud of their locomotives, for motive power was…the heart of the railway. [The locomotives were] named after Queens, Princesses, and famous regiments. But there was one omission, [the company] had not yet named locomotives after schools.' He then posed the question: 'Would you like to have your own locomotive – an engine named after your school?' This generous offer was quickly accepted for the school by Governor Mr Geoffrey Dawson (Editor of *The Times*). Around four months elapsed before no. 5538 *Giggleswick* was presented to the pupils at Settle station on 6th November 1938. Photograph courtesy *Yorkshire Post Newspapers*.

Opposite above NO. 5538 – PENMAENMAWR

Patriot Class no. 5538 is westbound at Penmaenmawr (on the North Wales Coast) with a Chester to Holyhead express. Not named at this time, the date is between construction at Crewe in July 1933 and when the plates were fitted in 1938.

Opposite below NO. 5543 – BRINKLOW

East of Coventry at Brinklow on 23rd September 1937, Patriot Class no. 5543 has the southbound 'Lancastrian' express. This had been a long-standing service, yet only found a title in 1928. The train ran from Manchester London Road to Euston and usually had 12 carriages in the formation which appears to be the case behind no. 5543. The northern departure time was 12.05 and a call was made at Stockport to attach 'through' portions from other locations. Another pause occurred at Macclesfield, then again at 13.10 for Stoke-on-Trent passengers. The remaining 145 miles to Euston were then run non-stop at 60 m.p.h. for termination at Euston around 15.40. This route was slightly different to the northbound train and meant a Patriot or Jubilee had to haul the coaches, whereas a Royal Scot usually had the 18.00 to Manchester. Photograph by T.G. Hepburn from Rail Archive Stephenson courtesy Rail-Online.

NO. 5544 – GLASGOW CENTRAL STATION
A smoky start is made by Patriot Class no. 5544 as the engine moves off (sanders on) with an express from Glasgow Central station in August 1938. Photograph courtesy Colour-Rail.

Above NO. 5549 – GRAYRIGG

To the north east of Kendal, Patriot no. 5549 has climbed from Oxenholme to Grayrigg with a Glasgow-bound excursion in July 1934. The engine has a reserve of steam for the next section up to Shap summit.

Below NO. 5547 – BRINKLOW

Around Nationalisation, Patriot no. 5547 has an express at Brinklow. Built at Crewe Works in April 1934, the engine was in traffic to September 1962. Throughout this period, no name was applied to the locomotive. Photograph courtesy Rail-Online.

Above NO. 6200

In the early 1930s, Stanier realised that a Pacific was necessary for increasing train weights and quickly developed a design which owed a debt of influence to the GWR King Class 4-6-0. The first LMSR Pacific was built at Crewe in June 1933 and is seen here at Euston station on 28th June 1933 still in works grey livery and unnamed. By mid-summer, the locomotive had been christened *The Princess Royal* and was in traffic wearing standard Crimson Lake livery.

Opposite above NO. 6201 – CREWE STATION

In nearly ex-works condition, Princess Royal Class Pacific no. 6201 *Princess Elizabeth* has reported for duty at Crewe station in late summer 1947. The engine has the post-war gloss black livery with pale-yellow lining and Sans Serif numbers and lettering. Photograph by W.H. Whitworth from Rail Archive Stephenson courtesy Rail-Online.

Opposite below NO. 6202 – SHREWSBURY STATION

As with high-pressure boilers, turbine drive, in place of reciprocating motion, offered increased efficiency and reduced component wear over a standard steam locomotive. In 1933, Stanier stepped boldly towards the feature and the third Princess Royal Pacific was selected as prototype. No. 6202 did not reach completion until 1935 and also had a modified boiler. The engine is at Shrewsbury station in the late 1930s.

Above **NO. 6204**

A young lad is shown round Princess Royal Pacific no. 6204 *Princess Louise* in 1938. The footplateman is perhaps explaining that the first two class members had GWR-type slide bars but these proved problematic in service. On the production engines they were replaced by a sturdy support bracket and shorter slidebars. The mechanical lubricators were also simplified to 12-feed rather than the 16-feed used initially. Contrary to GWR practice for the King Class 4-6-0s, the four cylinders of the Princess Royal Class engines had four sets of motion instead of the inside gear operating the outside via rocking levers. The cylinder layout was the same, with the inside pair far forward and the outside set back, but differed with slightly uneven length connecting rods and the outside cylinders inclined at 1 in 35.

Opposite above **NO. 6203 – OXENHOLME**

Three Stanier Pacifics were authorised for construction in 1933. Two of these appeared in July and November of the year, whilst a third was selected to trial a steam turbine drive. Initial experience with no. 6200 and no. 6201 determined an improved boiler was necessary owing to a too small superheater and non-optimal boiler proportions. When the second batch of nine Princess Royal Pacifics appeared in the second half of 1935 the boiler was much changed and had two variations – 24-element superheater and 32-element version. No. 6203 *Princess Margaret Rose* was built with the first mentioned in July 1935. The locomotive is in nearly-new condition passing Oxenholme with the northbound 'Royal Scot' around this time. Photograph by F.R. Hebron from Rail Archive Stephenson courtesy Rail-Online.

Opposite below **NO. 6205 – KINGS LANGLEY**

In the general naming scheme for express trains in the late 1920s, the 'premier' service between Euston and Liverpool was given the 'Merseyside Express' title. The northbound train left the capital in the early evening, whilst that leaving Liverpool departed around 10.00 and had to run from Mossley Hill non-stop at a mile-a-minute. Arrival at Euston was scheduled at 13.30. No. 6205 *Princess Victoria* is approaching the end of the journey, passing Kings Langley, just north of Watford, with the 'Merseyside Express' during 1938. Photograph by C.R.L. Coles from Rail Archive Stephenson courtesy Rail-Online.

Above **NO. 6206 – WATFORD JUNCTION**

No. 6206 *Marie Louise* passes Watford Junction with the 'Midday Scot' on 22nd April 1939. The introduction of the Princess Royal Pacifics resulted in changes to the service. When the Royal Scots were at the head of the train, the engine was switched at Crewe, yet from the mid-1930s the Princess Royals ran through from Euston to Glasgow. When the 'Coronation Scot' began in 1937, the 'Midday Scot' lost the official title, yet continued to leave Euston at 14.00 and run northward to Glasgow in 7 hours 55 minutes. Photograph by George C. Lander courtesy Rail Photoprints.

Below **NO. 6207 – SHREWSBURY STATION**

Princess Royal Pacific no. 6207 *Princess Arthur of Connaught* was built at Crewe Works in August 1935 and by the end of the month had found employment at Camden depot. Following a heavy repair in August 1938, the engine was kept at Crewe shed for a month and this is likely the period no. 6207 was seen at Shrewsbury station. Part of Collett Hall Class 4-6-0 no. 5946 *Marwell Hall* is visible to the left. Photograph courtesy Rail-Online.

© T.G. Hepburn/

Above NO. 6209 – CREWE WORKS

Around five days away from completion at Crewe Works, no. 6209 *Princess Beatrice* has been pictured on 18th August 1935. New to Camden depot, the engine was primarily allocated there to May 1942 when starting a long association with Crewe North shed. Photograph from Rail Archive Stephenson courtesy Rail-Online.

Opposite above NO. 6208 – RUGBY STATION

Though the LMSR and LNER had an unofficial non-competition agreement for their premier main line service – 'Royal Scot' and 'Flying Scotsman' respectively – this was dissolved in 1928. In the spirit of friendly rivalry, just before the LNER introduced the non-stop 'Flying Scotsman' in 1928, the LMSR ran the 'Royal Scot' non-stop between Euston-Glasgow and Euston-Edinburgh the week before. Yet, the company decided to return to a stop at Carlisle in order to split the two Scottish portions. During the winter months, the 'Royal Scot' made another two stops at Rugby and Crewe. The first-mentioned pause has taken place in late 1935, with no. 6208 *Princess Elena Victoria* eager to continue northward. Photograph by T.G. Hepburn from Rail Archive Stephenson courtesy Rail-Online.

Opposite below NO. 6210 – BROCK WATER TROUGHS

Around seven miles north of Preston, Brock water troughs were laid in the 1860s and stretched over 500 yards along the WCML. A southbound express is crossing over the troughs in May 1936. The engine is no. 6210 *Lady Patricia* and at this time was still paired with an original 4,000-gallon tender with space for 9 tons of coal. The class later upgraded to a new tender with larger coal space capable of securing 10 tons of coal. No. 6210 was soon to switch in September and remained with the type – though different examples – to withdrawal in October 1961. Photograph courtesy Rail Photoprints.

JUBILEE

Above NO. 5552
In the early 1940s, Jubilee Class 4-6-0 no. 5552 *Silver Jubilee* is serviced. The locomotive has wartime black livery yet retains the special chrome numbers and lettering fitted in 1935.

Opposite above NO. 6211
The penultimate Princess Royal Pacific in traffic was no. 6211 *Queen Maud* during mid-September 1935. The engine was new to Camden and primarily resided there to 1943. No. 6211 is in nearly new condition here during late 1935. The locomotive was amongst the latter group built with a boiler possessing 32-element superheater, which later became standard under British Railways, along with dome regulator. A feature of both 24-element and 32-element boilers was a larger firebox combustion chamber which differentiated the first two boilers with the later ones in extending further forward to the centre of the rear coupled wheel. Photograph courtesy Rail-Online.

Opposite below NO. 6212
The Princess Royal Class had 6 ft 6 in. diameter driving wheels compared to the 6 ft 9 in. of the later Coronation Class Pacifics. Nos 6200-6212 had tyres fastened to the wheel centres using Gibson rings, which were invented by J. Gibson of the GWR. The process of this saw the centre lowered into the red hot tyre and the Gibson ring rolled over at the rear to secure the pair together. This went on to improve the reliability of LMSR tyres. The balance weights consisted of two plates riveted together and the required lead filled the space between. Molybdenum steel was used for coupling and connecting rods, whilst only the latter were fluted. A wheeltapper is depicted checking for fatigue in the tyres belonging to no. 6212 *Duchess of Kent* in the late 1930s.

Above NO. 5638 – CATHIRON

The West Coast Main Line passed through the village of Cathiron, around three miles north of Rugby. With two roads crossing over, there were vantage points for enthusiasts to record events over the years. On 25th May 1939, no. 5638 *Zanzibar* is viewed from Cathiron Lane travelling southward with a mixed train. Around three months earlier, the locomotive had returned to traffic following an overhaul which saw the improved boiler fitted. When pictured, no. 5638 was on the roster at Crewe North depot. Photograph from the David P. Williams Archive courtesy Rail-Online.

Below NO. 5565

Whilst the Royal Scots and the Princess Royal Pacifics capably handled the top expresses, support was needed in several areas. Stanier designed the Class 5XP 4-6-0 and a large initial order was placed at the North British Locomotive Company, as well as Crewe, with some from Derby. The construction period spanned just two years, 1934-1936, when 191 examples were built. The boiler design was revised around half-way through and the class became good, reliable performers for the LMSR and successor London Midland Region of British Railways. No. 5565 was built by the NBLC's Hyde Park Works in August 1934 and was new to Preston. The engine is pictured with footplatemen and guard around 1936/1937 when named *Victoria* following the Commonwealth theme adopted for the class during George V's Jubilee year 1935. The locomotive also left Preston for Blackpool in May 1937.

Above NO. 5737 – TRING SUMMIT
No. 5737 *Atlas* has reached Tring summit with a London Euston to Birmingham New Street express in 1939. Photograph from the Dave Cobbe Collection courtesy Rail Photoprints.

Below NO. 5742
Several Jubilee Class engines carried double chimneys of varying types during their lifespan. No. 5742 *Connaught* was fitted in 1940 and this was present to 1955.

CORONATION

Above **CORONATION PACIFIC – CREWE WORKS**

In the early 20th century, few attempts were made to convey passengers quickly between places. British East Coast and West Coast companies actually held an unofficial arrangement where London to Scotland times were held at eight hours to ward off competition. In the late 1920s, the Depression and developments in Europe and America saw high-speed lightly-loaded trains favoured in order to keep and entice passengers that might have been otherwise lured away to emerging forms of transport – the motor car and the aeroplane. Whilst these might not have been pressing concerns in 1930s Britain – certainly by the 1950s cars and lorries were decimating the railways – the rise of publicity departments influenced the decision to adopt such services. The London & North Eastern Railway was first to offer the 'Silver Jubilee' streamlined train between Newcastle and King's Cross in 1935 and for the 1937 summer season, the 'Coronation' from King's Cross to Edinburgh in six hours was ready for service. The LMSR had taken notice of the 'Silver Jubilee' and ran tests for a high-speed Euston to Glasgow train in late 1936. An improved version of the Princess Royal Pacific was designed specially for the new 'Coronation Scot' express and featured streamlining which was used in varying degrees across Europe and America. The LNER A4 Pacific used on the 'Silver Jubilee' had been tested at the National Physical Laboratory for aerodynamic efficiency, whilst the streamlining for the new LMSR Pacific was also determined in a wind tunnel at Derby. An initial order for five Coronation Pacifics was completed at Crewe Works in 1937 and a second order appeared before the streamlining was discontinued for a time only to be taken up again later. A streamlined Pacific is in the process of being wheeled here at Crewe Works.

Above NO. 6223 – CAMDEN
No. 6223 *Princess Alice* has reached the top of Camden incline with the 'Coronation Scot' express during the 1930s. The first batch of five had a special blue livery which matched the train.

Below NO. 6220 – CREWE WORKS
The workers at Crewe welcome no. 6220 *Coronation* into service around late May 1937.

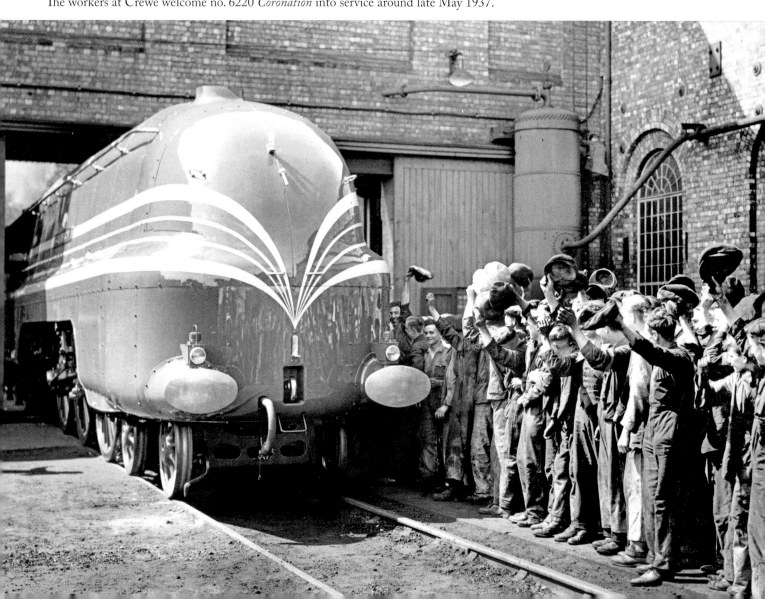

Above NO. 6240

No. 6240 *City of Coventry* is likely at Camden shed being cleaned and serviced in 1943. The engine was completed at Crewe in March 1940 and was at Camden from April to September 1963.

Above **NO. 6220**

Following in the footsteps of Royal Scot Class no. 6100 *Royal Scot*, no. 6220 *Coronation* was sent to America in 1939. This was for a short tour – still totalling 3,000 miles – along the East Coast, then taking a position at the World's Fair in New York. The engine departed from Southampton early in the year and during the course of the visit, the Second World War started. Initially, the Baltimore & Ohio Railroad stored the engine and carriages, though the motive power was later deemed necessary and no. 6220 crossed the Atlantic successfully in 1942.

Opposite above **NO. 6220 – HARTFORD**

No. 6220 *Coronation* is at Hartford, USA, on display, 14th April 1939. Around two weeks remained to the opening of the World's Fair on 30th April and the end date was 27th October 1940 when 44 million people had visited. Also on display was the Pennsylvania Railroad's S1 Class 'Duplex' 6-4-4-6 experimental locomotive which had a streamlined casing designed by Raymond Loewy and had a resemblance to the Coronation Pacific. Impressively, the S1 was on rollers and ran daily, reaching 60 m.p.h. while stationary. Photograph from Rail Archive Stephenson courtesy Rail-Online.

Opposite below **NO. 6220**

The principal train on the Baltimore & Ohio Railroad was the 'Royal Blue' which ran from New York City to Washington D.C. This had been in service from 1890 and ran with various names to 1935 when taking 'Royal Blue'. In 1937, a P7 Class Pacific was rebuilt with streamlining and others later followed. No. 5304 *President Monroe* was the locomotive and when no. 6220 visited the opportunity was taken to picture the pair together. This occurred on the Thomas Viaduct near Elkridge, Maryland, crossing the Patapsco River and Valley.

Above NO. 6250

In 1939 a further 20 Coronation Pacifics were ordered by the LMSR. Yet, with the outbreak of war towards the end of the year, materials and manpower were soon turned towards the military build-up. The locomotives did appear in sporadic batches of four to five a year over the period 1943-1948. Whilst the first lot of four in 1943 had streamlining, during 1944 this was discontinued and the Pacifics had a normal appearance. No. 6250 was the second of four to appear in 1944. From the late 1930s the naming policy had switched to cities and the locomotive was *City of Lichfield* from June 1944 when a ceremony occurred at Lichfield station on the 20th.

Opposite CORONATION PACIFIC

The disadvantages of providing four sets of valve gear included the restricted space in between the frames, increased number of oiling points and complicated nature of the arrangement. Following experience with the Princess Royals, the LMSR decided to take up the option initially rejected of using the outside valve gear and rocking levers to operate the inside valves of the Coronation Pacifics. Their fear was that valve spindle expansion would cause unequal valve events but with careful design this was kept to a minimum as a trade-off between the disadvantages of the two arrangements. The coupling and connecting rods were manufactured using 'Vibrac' steel, which had been developed in the early 1920s by Armstrong Whitworth & Co. to not become brittle during tempering. An engineman is seen oiling the big end of the connecting rod of an unidentified Coronation Pacific.

DIESEL

Above **DIESEL RAILCAR**
By the 1930s, diesel propulsion was finding favour on railways in Europe and America. Early in the decade, the 'Flying Hamburger' diesel railcar achieved fame running between Berlin and Hamburg. In the mid-1930s, the LMSR decided to take up a similar idea and a three-coach diesel railcar was built at Derby in 1939. This had seating for 162 and six engines providing a total of 750 horsepower. Initially the railcar found use between Oxford and Cambridge, then on the Midland Main Line to Nottingham. Withdrawn in 1939, the railcar did not return to service.

Opposite above **NO. 1012**
Johnson 1000 Class 4-4-0 three-cylinder compound no. 1012 has an express on the Midland Main Line near Derby in the 1930s. The locomotive was one of 45 erected at Derby Works, being completed in December 1905.

Opposite below **NO. 1045**
Fowler was keen to continue with the 4-4-0 compound after Grouping and 195 examples appeared from 1924-1932. No. 1045 was the first built at Derby Works in February 1924 and was similar to the preceding Johnson 1000 Class, but had slightly smaller driving wheels at 6ft 9in. compared with 7ft.

PASSENGER TENDER LOCOMOTIVES

NO. 1048

Fowler Compound 4-4-0 no. 1048 was constructed at Derby Works in March 1924. The locomotive was in service to October 1957, working at several locations along the Midland Main Line.

Above NO. 1088 – KENTISH TOWN SHED
Fowler Compound no. 1088 was one of 20 class members erected by the ex-Lancashire & Yorkshire works at Horwich. The engine is at Kentish Town in the mid- to late 1920s with company crest on the cab and number on the tender.

Below NO. 1061
An interesting image where Fowler Compound no. 1061 has been paired with the tender belonging to class mate no. 1050. This occurred on several instances and likely reinforced the need to switch company branding from the cab to tender. The locomotive was new from Derby in June 1924 whilst no. 1050 had left the same works three months earlier.

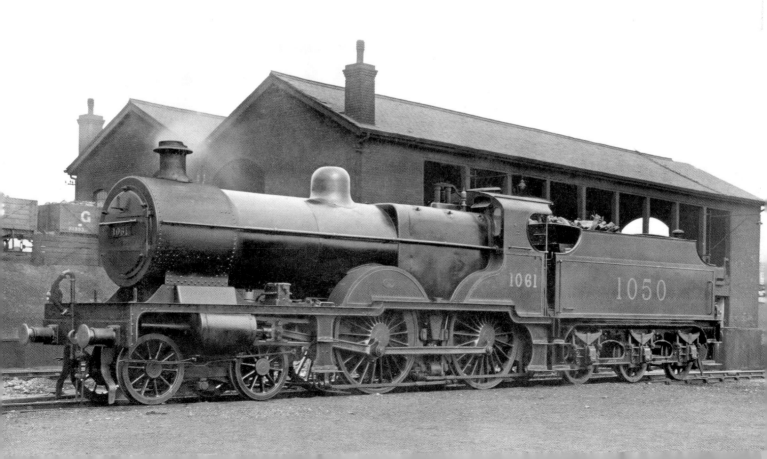

NO. 1141 AND NO. 14358 – CARLISLE

Fowler Compound no. 1141 has teamed with J.F. McIntosh 140 (Dunalastair IV) Class 4-4-0 no. 14358 to take the Edinburgh portion of a Euston to Glasgow express northward towards the late 1920s.

Above NO. 1137 – WATFORD JUNCTION STATION

On 10th June 1939, Fowler Compound no. 1137 is bound for Euston through Watford Junction station. Photograph by George C. Lander courtesy Rail Photoprints.

Below NO. 1152 – CAMDEN

Fowler Compound no. 1152 has paused at Camden for this image to be captured around the late 1920s. North British Locomotive Company-built, the engine has a diamond-shaped Queen's Park Works plate on the driving wheel splasher. No. 1152 was new in September 1925.

Below **NO. 641 – DUMFRIES SHED**

The Midland Railway had a long line of 4-4-0s and Fowler updated the design in the late 1920s for intermediate passenger duties. The new 2P Class 4-4-0s had higher boiler pressure, slightly larger cylinder diameter and 6ft 9in. diameter driving wheels. In just four years, 1928-1932, 138 locomotives were built, mainly at Derby, but some came from Crewe Works. No. 641 emerged from the latter in August 1931 and is seen at Dumfries shed.

Above NO. 650 – GLASGOW ST ENOCH STATION

An ambitious plan to link all the railway lines entering Glasgow was formulated by the City of Glasgow Union Railway in the early 1860s. This did not find favour with all companies, yet the project progressed to completion in 1870. A main feature of the scheme was a station at St Enoch Square, the construction of which took several years and did not welcome traffic until 1876. There were six platforms covered by a glass train shed 198 ft wide and 504 ft long. Subsequently, the Glasgow & South Western Railway took over St Enoch station and entered a partnership with the Midland Railway to accept trains from England. St Enoch was in use to 1966 and later demolished. Fowler 2P Class 4-4-0 no. 650 arrives at St Enoch station with a local train in 1933. Photograph courtesy Rail Photoprints.

Above NO. 633

The efficiency of the locomotive was always a concern for locomotive engineers and a number of new appliances to improve fuel/water consumption, maintenance, etc. were always on hand for testing over the years. One aspect of reducing coal consumption was using the exhaust steam to pre-heat the feedwater before entering the boiler. Several systems were developed for this and one was the Dabeg feedwater heater which mixed the exhaust steam and feedwater in apparatus on the running plate. The pump was driven by a connection to an axle. Two Fowler Class 2P 4-4-0s were equipped in the 1930s, no. 633 and 653. The first mentioned has been pictured to document the fitting in 1933. Built at Derby in 1928, the locomotive was sold soon after to the Somerset & Dorset Joint Railway but returned to LMSR stock in 1930. The Dabeg equipment persisted with no. 633 to the 1950s.

Opposite NO. 667 – PAISLEY GILMOUR STREET STATION

Fowler 2P Class no. 667 has an express on the through line at Paisley Gilmour Street station on 1st August 1938. Two railway companies came together to open a joint station at Paisley in the late 1830s. The Glasgow, Paisley & Greenock and Glasgow, Paisley, Kilmarnock & Ayr Railways laid a single line from Glasgow to Paisley where they split to reach their respective destinations. Gilmour Street station was opened in 1840, with the GPK&AR company advanced enough to begin running trains, whilst the other was not ready until the following year. By the end of the decade, both companies were part of the Glasgow & South Western Railway and Caledonian Railway respectively. In the 1880s the station was expanded from two platforms to four. Photograph by Les Hanson from the David Hanson Archive courtesy Rail-Online.

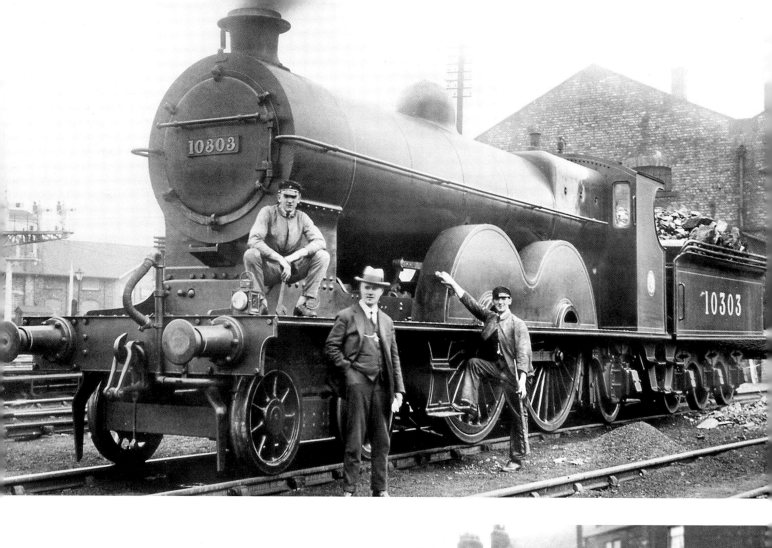

Above **NO. 5113 – BARROW-IN-FURNESS STATION**
No. 5113 began life as an F.W. Webb Jubilee Class 4-4-0 four-cylinder compound, no. 1912 *Colossus*. Built in June 1899, the locomotive was later rebuilt in May 1924 under George Whale and joined the Renown Class as a two-cylinder simple engine. Also renumbered 5113 at this time, the engine survived just another five years before scrapped. During this period, no. 5113 is pictured at Barrow-in-Furness station.

Opposite above **NO. 10303 – YORK QUEEN STREET SHED**
Interestingly, the LMSR inherited just one class of 4-4-2 'Atlantic' locomotive, whereas all of the major East Coast companies had the type dominating. The Lancashire & Yorkshire Railway bequeathed J. Aspinall's Class 7 at Grouping and this consisted of 40 engines built between 1899 and 1902. No. 10303 was an early example, appearing from Horwich in April 1899. The locomotive poses with crew and official at York Queen Street shed in the mid-1920s. The Midland Railway had stabling facilities at York thanks to the York & North Midland Railway. These were located at the south end of the station, as were lines for servicing other 'foreign' locomotives at a building formerly belonging to the Y&NMR workshops. The Great Central, Great Eastern and Lancashire & Yorkshire Railways all used this area up to Grouping. The ex-MR depot was taken over by the LNER, whilst visiting LMSR locomotives moved over to the ex-workshop area at Queen Street and used this to 1932 when a new building was provided in the middle of the running lines and sidings a short distance away. No. 10303 was in service to April 1927 when condemned.

Opposite below **NO. 733 – SHEFFIELD MIDLAND STATION**
In the early 20th century, S.W. Johnson introduced an improved express passenger 4-4-0. The design also saw the MR move towards the Belpaire firebox. A total of 80 were erected from 1900 to 1905, including no. 733 in 1903. The engine has a local train at Sheffield Midland station, likely in the early 1930s. No. 733 survived to September 1936.

Above NO. 5389

Charles Bowen-Cooke introduced a new superheated 4-4-0 in 1910 at the time of the accession of George V, inspiring the name for the new class. Ninety appeared up to 1915, including no. 5389 which was the product of Crewe in April 1913 and named *Eclipse*. The engine was in service to June 1937.

Below NO. 12459 – NEWTON HEATH SHED

Aspinall Class 11 0-6-0 no. 12459 is in the yard at Newton Heath depot in 1931.

Above NO. 5910 – CREWE NORTH SHED

The Claughton Class 4-6-0 was introduced by Charles Bowen-Cooke in 1913 and construction continued to just before Grouping, with 130 locomotives built. No. 5910 *J.A. Bright* was an early example, appearing in August 1914. On 4th July 1934, the locomotive is at Crewe shed. Photograph by T.G. Hepburn courtesy Rail-Online.

Below NO. 6017 – HEADSTONE LANE

A Camden to Walsall goods passes Headstone Lane with Claughton no. 6017 *Breadalbane* during 1939. Photograph by C.R.L. Coles from Rail Archive Stephenson courtesy Rail-Online.

PASSENGER TANKS

Above **NO. 16580 – GANWICK**

Fowler 3F 0-6-0T no. 16580 is northbound towards Potters Bar at Ganwick, c. 1930. A large number of class members were concentrated at Devons Road, Bow, for North London Railway suburban services from Broad Street, taking the East Coast Main Line up to Potters Bar. When not working these, the 3Fs could be seen on transfer freights around the capital, as well as shunting, which was the task the engines were intended. No. 16580 was built by the Vulcan Foundry in April 1928 and was a long-term servant at Devons Road. The locomotive later went to Carlisle and was at Birkenhead for a time before condemned during September 1962.

Opposite above **NO. 2300**

A powerful tank locomotive for medium-distance passenger services was required by the Operating Department in the mid-1920s. Fowler produced the 4P Class 2-6-4T which was the basis for several variations leading to Stanier, Fairburn and the BR Standard Classes. Fowler's engine was introduced in 1927 and produced up to 1934 when 125 were in service. No. 2300 was the first and ready from Derby Works in December. The engine is pictured likely in the 1930s with a local train.

Opposite below **NO. 2341 – NOTTINGHAM MIDLAND STATION**

Fowler 4P Class 2-6-4T no. 2341 is at Nottingham Midland station, c. 1930. The first fifteen locomotives appeared during a transition concerning liveries. Initially, Crimson Lake was applied with standard lining, but this soon changed to include only express passenger engines and the 4P 2-6-4Ts were given plain black with vermilion lining around the edges. No. 2341 was built at Derby in April 1929 and has the latter livery still presentable.

DOGSHEAD
BRAND

BOTTLED
BEERS

READ BROTHERS

BOTTLING STORES

15830

Above NO. 28 – KENTISH TOWN SHED

The Midland Railway initially reached London via the courtesy of the London & Birmingham Railway, then when the relationship soured the Great Northern Railway allowed running powers. Line capacity soon saw the MR construct a new line to London and when this opened in the late 1860s, a new depot was built at Kentish Town. A major construction project improved the stabling at the turn of the century and this included a large double coaling stage, which is seen here behind Fowler 3P Class 2-6-2T no. 28. The stage was soon to be lost as the LMSR organised works to build a mechanical coaler and ash disposal facilities in 1939 and 1940. No. 28 was originally no. 15527 and renumbering occurred in May 1934. Photograph courtesy Rail Photoprints.

Opposite NO. 15530 – KENTISH TOWN SHED

Whilst the 4P 2-6-4T served a purpose, a similar locomotive with wider route availability was needed. Fowler initially planned an 0-6-2T, which was in line with LNER preference, before choosing a 2-6-2T design for better weight distribution. The 3P Class was introduced in 1930 and 70 were constructed at Derby Works in just two years. No. 15530 appeared in March 1931 and in May 1934 was renumbered 31. The engine is in the yard at Kentish Town shed on 2nd September 1933 with two forebears – a Johnson 0-4-4T and a Kirtley 0-4-4WT. All are condenser-fitted for working the London suburban trains. Photograph by T.G. Hepburn from Rail Archive Stephenson courtesy Rail-Online.

Above NO. 6408 – WATFORD JUNCTION STATION

The Midland Railway had a number of 0-4-4T classes, but the last was S.W. Johnson's 2228 Class built up to the early 20th century. The Caledonian Railway also constructed several with the final W. Pickersgill 159 and 431 Class members appearing around Grouping. Despite other types finding favour, ten new 0-4-4Ts were designed around the time of Stanier's appointment, being slightly more powerful than their predecessors. No. 6408 was part of this small batch of locomotives and was erected at Derby Works in December 1932. At Watford Junction station on 10th June 1939, some class members worked locally on the branch to St Albans. No. 6408 was renumbered 1908 just before Nationalisation and was in service to November 1959. Photograph by George C. Lander courtesy Rail Photoprints.

Opposite above NO. 71

In works grey livery, Stanier 3P Class 2-6-2T no. 71 stands newly constructed at Derby in 1935. The design was a development of Fowler's 2-6-2T, with a new boiler, cab and self-trimming coal bunker. The first two batches had a domeless boiler, then from 1937 a domed boiler was used. No. 71 was the first class member in traffic during February 1935.

Opposite below NO. 90 – ELSTREE

Emerging from the 1,050-yard-long Elstree tunnel on 3rd July 1937 is Stanier 3P no. 90. The locomotive is at the head of a local train. At the time, no. 90 had been in traffic two years and would be active for another 25, being condemned in July 1962. Sixty-nine Stanier 3Ps were in service at the start of the year, though all had gone by the end of 1962.

Above NO. 155 – POTTERS BAR
From no. 145 built at Derby in 1937, the Stanier 3Ps had a modified boiler with increased heating surfaces, dome-mounted regulator and separate top feed. No. 155 has the new boiler at Potters Bar on 13th May 1939, whilst also featuring the late 1930s Sans Serif front numberplate. The locomotive is southbound with a Broad Street train. Photograph by George C. Lander courtesy Rail Photoprints.

Opposite above NO. 137 – MOTHERWELL STATION
On 2nd August 1938, Stanier 3P Class no. 137 arrives at Motherwell station with an express. In October 1935, the locomotive was new to the local depot, though by Nationalisation had left for Llandudno. Apart from a spell at Nuneaton in the early 1950s, no. 137 was in the North West until condemned during November 1962. Motherwell station was the second to serve the town, replacing a facility sited a distance away. In the 1970s, British Railways rebuilt Motherwell as part of the WCML electrification. Photograph by Les Hanson from the David Hanson Archive courtesy Rail-Online.

Opposite below NO. 143
A local train is at an unidentified location with Stanier 3P no. 143 in the late 1930s. Perhaps the main duty for the class was stopping trains, though employment was also found on empty stock movements and banking on inclines.

Above NO. 2535 – PLAISTOW SHED

Four Stanier 4P 2-6-4T locomotives are in the yard at Plaistow shed during November 1935. Stanier designed a three-cylinder 4P 2-6-4T specifically for the London, Tilbury & Southend line in 1934 as he thought the extra cylinder would provide an advantage in starting off and keeping on schedule. This was not realised but the class continued to be used on the route, as well as further afield. Around ten were based at Plaistow shed over the years. No. 2535 is on the turntable, with both enginemen moving the locomotive, whilst no. 2530, no. 252X and no. 2527 are also present. Photograph courtesy Rail Photoprints.

Opposite above NO. 2448 – DERBY WORKS

The North Midland Railway established Derby Works in 1840. The early facilities were used for repair before first Locomotive Superintendent of the Midland Railway Matthew Kirtley turned to new construction. The pioneer locomotive built at Derby was 0-6-0 no. 147 in 1851. By Grouping, the site covered nearly 130 acres on the east side of the station, with employment for over 3,000. Under the LMSR, the shops lost some importance with locomotive construction but continued to contribute Royal Scots, Patriots, 0-6-0s, 2-6-4Ts and 2-6-2Ts, etc. There were also improvements in repair practices and the number of engines congregated for attention was reduced. Twenty general repairs were completed weekly. Stanier 4P Class no. 2448 is in for attention during March 1938. The engine had been completed at Derby almost two years earlier.

Opposite below DERBY WORKS

Derby Works had a close association with the 2-6-4T type, from Fowler's version, through Stanier's 4P and Charles Fairburn's final development. Nearly 500 appeared from the works between 1927 and 1950. During the mid-1940s, a 2-6-4T – possibly an early Fairburn 4P – is in the Erecting Shop at Derby.

Above NO. 1327 – NOTTINGHAM MIDLAND STATION
Johnson 1532 Class 0-4-4T no. 1327 has a local service at Nottingham Midland station during 1934. The engine was built in May 1886 and survived to early 1940.

Below NO. 1381 – KENTISH TOWN SHED
In the yard at Kentish Town shed is Johnson 2228 Class no. 1381.

Above NO. 2128 – GRAYS STATION

Derby-built London, Tilbury & Southend Railway T. Whitelegg 79 Class 4-4-2T no. 2128 is at Grays station, c. 1930. The LTSR built just four, with the remaining 35 engines erected under the LMSR.

Below NO. 10899 – DONCASTER STATION

Ex-L&YR Aspinall 1008 Class 2-4-2T no. 10899 has a local train, likely from Wakefield/Pontefract at Doncaster station in the 1930s. The engine was erected at Horwich in April 1910 and ran to October 1948.

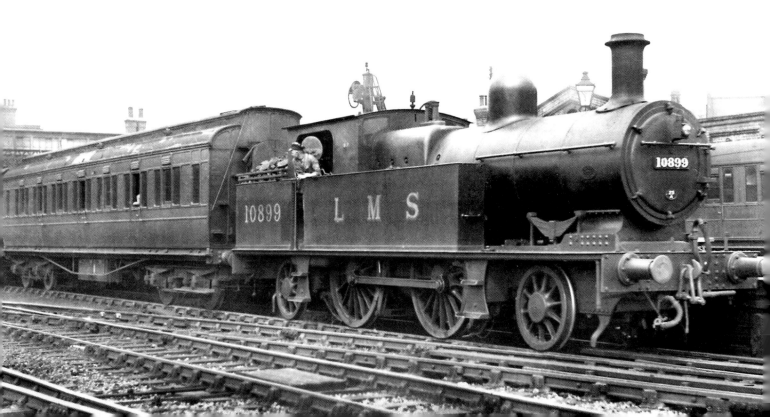

RAILMOTOR

Above NO. 10616 – WAKEFIELD SHED
Many railway companies attempted to cut costs by using railcars and railmotors on local lines. The L&YR built 18 at Horwich between 1906-1911, with one of the last being no. 10616. Latterly, the railmotor was used between Wakefield and Edlington, near Doncaster. No. 10616 is pictured at Wakefield shed, c. 1930.

Below NO. 13030
Hughes 'Crab' Class 2-6-0 no. 13030 posed with crew, c. 1930. Later in the decade, the locomotive was renumbered 2730.

MIXED TRAFFIC

Above NO. 13074
Shortly after Grouping, George Hughes produced a design for a mixed traffic 2-6-0. Up to 1934 245 'Crab' Class locomotives were constructed at Horwich and Crewe. No. 13074, which has an express, was new in August 1927 and has the original application of number to the tender. This went on to be discontinued from early 1928.

Below NO. 2766 – SHEFFIELD MIDLAND STATION
No. 2766 has an express at Sheffield Midland station in the late 1930s.

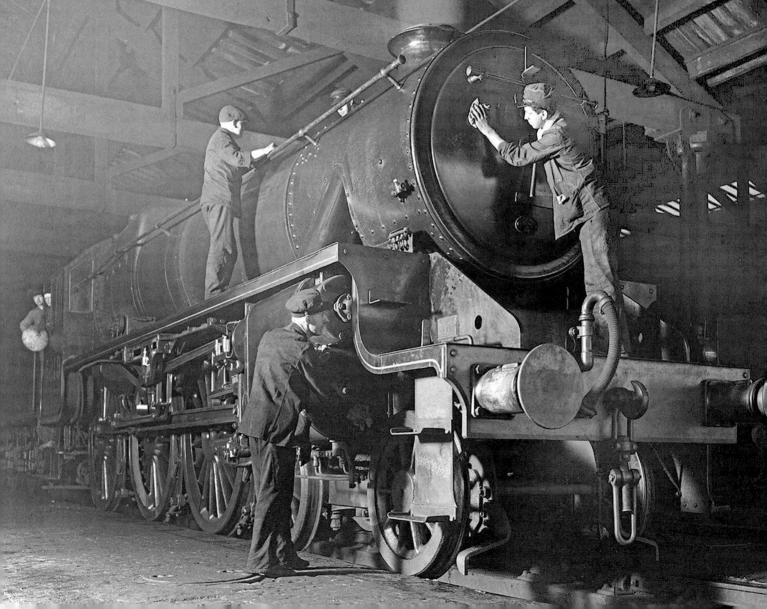

Above NO. 5037 – HUDDERSFIELD SHED

The LMSR made improvements at Huddersfield shed in 1937 and these kept the depot running to closure in 1967. Perhaps installed at this time is the vacuum motor for moving the turntable which was from Cowans Sheldon as advertised on the board behind the engineman. The LMSR had first adopted the technology two years earlier. Stanier Class 5 no. 5037 is also illustrated.

Opposite above NO. 13245

One of Stanier's early designs was a new version of Hughes' 'Crab' 2-6-0. No. 13245 was the first of 40 produced in 1933/1934 and is pictured when new in works grey livery.

Opposite below NO. 5218

Stanier Class 5 4-6-0 no. 5218 is under the attention of cleaners in the late 1930s. The engine was amongst 100 ordered from Armstrong Whitworth & Co. in 1935. Another 227 would appear from the company in the following two years.

Below NO. 5016 – LOCHGORM WORKS

The first 20 Stanier Class 5 4-6-0s were constructed at Crewe Works in 1935. No. 5016 entered traffic in May and had a domeless boiler, with a straight throatplate firebox and 14-element superheater. Experience with the class saw improvements made to the boiler design and a dome-mounted regulator was provided, later fireboxes had a sloping throatplate, whilst the size of the superheater was increased. No. 5016 is suspended above the wheels at Lochgorm Works on 9th June 1937. The LMSR inherited the facilities at Inverness from the Highland Railway at Grouping. The shops had been established in the 1850s by the Inverness & Nairn Railway and did construct locomotives for a time but concentrated on repairs from the early 20th century. Photograph by L.R. Tomsett from Rail Archive Stephenson courtesy Rail-Online.

Above NO. 5344 – BRINKLOW

On 23rd September 1937, no. 5344 had been in traffic around five months and is already quite work-worn. The engine was dispatched from Armstrong Whitworth & Co. with black livery with vermillion lining and bright metal work, including smokebox door hinges, motion, wheel rims, etc. At the time, the LMSR had also changed number and lettering style to Sans Serif which is prominent on the door plate, whilst cab and tender transfers are nearly obscured. No. 5344 has a southbound freight at Brinklow (between Coventry and Rugby). Photograph by T.G. Hepburn from Rail Archive Stephenson courtesy Rail-Online.

Left and below NO. 6400

As an improvement on the 0-6-0 locomotives in service, H.G. Ivatt produced the Class 2MT 2-6-0 design in 1946. Twenty were built under the LMSR whilst 108 were constructed by British Railways. Thirty-eight appeared from Darlington Works for employment in the Eastern and North Eastern Regions, with another 25 for the Western Region erected at Swindon Works. No. 6400 was the first class member new from Crewe Works in December 1946 and featured a self-cleaning smokebox (the 'SC' on the front door), improved access to motion components and split running plate.

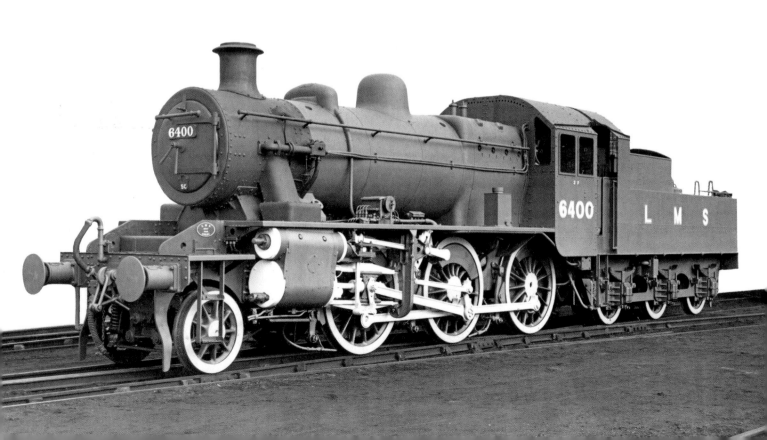

FREIGHT

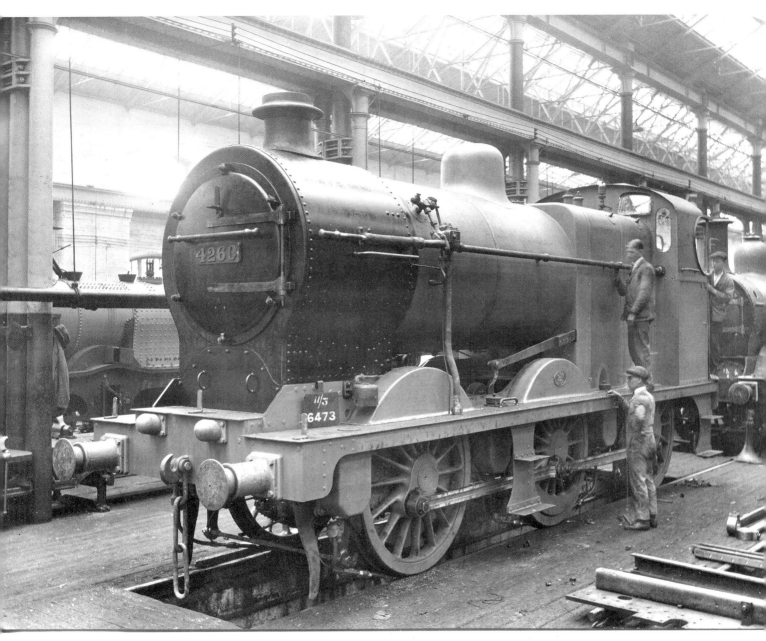

Above **NO. 4260 – DERBY WORKS**

Fowler established his 3835 Class 0-6-0 for the Midland Railway's freight duties in the decade before Grouping. For the LMSR, the design was thought suitable for the system and with slight differences 575 were built from 1924-1941. No. 4260 is under construction at Derby Works in 1926 as part of Lot no. 29 for 115 4F Class 0-6-0s. Several places were involved in erecting the 0-6-0s, including Crewe, Horwich and St Rollox, in addition to contractors, the NBLC, Andrew Barclay and Kerr, Stuart & Co. No. 4260 was in service for nearly 40 years, being condemned during October 1964.

Above NO. 4118 – STOKE-ON-TRENT SHED

Just to the south of Stoke-on-Trent station, the North Staffordshire Railway established locomotive servicing facilities in the late 1840s. The site later evolved to accommodate a roundhouse and straight shed. These were refurbished by the LMSR in the mid-1930s and just before the war, a mechanical coaler was erected. Fowler 4F no. 4118 poses next to the new coaler in the late 1930s.

Above NO. 9525

For mineral traffic on the Midland line, a new locomotive was needed in the late 1920s. Fowler took inspiration from the LNWR's Beames G2 Class 0-8-0 and produced the 7F 0-8-0. In just three years, 175 engines were built, including no. 9525 in June 1929.

Below NO. 9637 – CASTLETHORPE

Between Bletchley and Northampton on the WCML, Fowler 7F no. 9637 has a mixed freight passing over Castlethorpe water troughs. The locomotive was erected at Crewe in January 1932 and had a career spanning 30 years.

Above **NO. 8011 – CREWE WORKS**

Despite large numbers of 0-8-0s being in traffic, these were not particularly reliable owing to flaws in the design. When Stanier was appointed one of his priorities was a 2-8-0 for heavy freight traffic. Twelve 8F Class locomotives were ordered initially in 1933 and these were built at Crewe in 1935. No. 8011 was the last of this batch and is well on the way to completion here in the shops on 13th October. A total of 852 8Fs went on to be constructed, though only 331 were produced by the LMSR as the War Department ordered a large number in the Second World War, as did other railway companies to ease motive power shortages during the conflict. At Nationalisation, 624 were inherited by British Railways and the 8Fs served to the end of steam, with a number later preserved. Photograph by W. Leslie Good from Rail Archive Stephenson courtesy Rail-Online.

Opposite **STANIER 8F CLASS LOCOMOTIVES**

Six Stanier 8F Class 2-8-0s are lined up at an unidentified location in the early 1940s. The leading two engines are nos 8198 and 8199 which had been constructed by the NBLC in June 1942. At the outbreak of war a strain was placed on the country's locomotive stock as the LNER and GWR had to donate freight engines to the War Department whilst traffic also increased due to the movement of materials. As a result, the LMSR ordered 100 8F Class 2-8-0s from Crewe Works, yet this was later reduced to 50 with the remainder placed at the NBLC, which included nos 8198 and 8199. Next is no. 8105 and the engine was built at Crewe in February 1939 as part of an order dated May 1937. Standing behind is no. 564. Following the outbreak of war, the WD chose the 8F design for service and ordered over 200 and no. 564 was included, being completed by the NBLC in July 1942. Whilst many of these were soon dispatched overseas, no. 564, which has a WD number, some were loaned to the LMSR. This lasted nearly a year, but no. 564 was purchased by the LMSR at the end of 1943 and became no. 8277 and was in traffic to April 1966. The second to last engine appears to be no. 8001 but the last is unidentifiable.

Above **NO. 8066 – RATCLIFFE-ON-SOAR**

Happily steaming southward at Ratcliffe-on-Soar (south west of Nottingham) with a train of empty iron ore wagons is Stanier 8F no. 8066. Pictured on 19th May 1940, the locomotive was one of 51 requisitioned by the War Department in late 1941 for use in the Middle East as ordered locomotives were not yet complete. No. 8066 became WD no. 608 in October and was later dispatched in December on board the SS *Pentridge Hall*. Whilst in the Irish Sea, a storm threatened the vessel and to avert disaster no. 608, along with three other 8Fs, were deliberatley pushed in the water. Eight others being transported had to be repaired when the boat returned to port and ultimately remained in Britain. Photograph by J.P. Wilson from Rail Archive Stephenson courtesy Rail-Online.

Opposite **STANIER 8F CLASS LOCOMOTIVE**

A boilersmith emerges from the firebox of a Stanier 8F Class locomotive. Close attention was paid to the cabs for both the Class 5 4-6-0 and 8F 2-8-0, with the controls placed as near to the driver as possible. The screw reverser mechanism is on the left, the regulator is central on the firebox with long handle and the steam manifold is above. A maintenance device was later fitted above the firehole door where sand was shot towards the tubeplate to clean the tubes. No. 8096 was new with the feature, as were subsequent engines, in addition to earlier ones, though from 1952 removal started to occur.

GARRATT

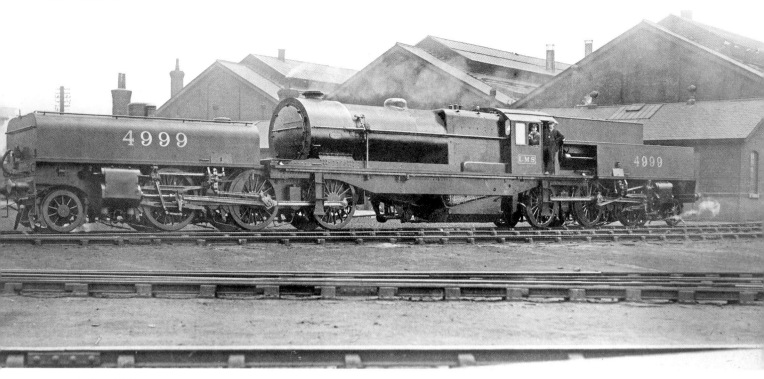

Above **NO. 4999**
Garratt 2-6-0+0-6-2 no. 4999 was built by Beyer Peacock & Co. in April 1927 as one of three introduced for the Nottinghamshire-London coal traffic on the Midland Main Line.

Below **NO. 4998 – CRICKLEWOOD SHED**
At Cricklewood shed is Garratt 2-6-0+0-6-2 no. 4998, which was the second of the trio built in 1927.

Above GARRATT – ELSTREE

An unidentified Garratt has a mixed freight at Elstree in 1935. In 1930, a further 30 locomotives of the type were erected by Beyer Peacock & Co. Photograph from the Dave Cobbe Collection courtesy Rail Photoprints.

Below NO. 7973 – CREWE WORKS

Though all Garratts were built with coal bunkers, from 1931 revolving coal bunkers were fitted to 31 of the 33 class members. No. 7973 was built as no. 4973 but this changed to allow Stanier Class 5 4-6-0s to take the Garratt sequence, no. 4967-4999. On 7th May 1939 no. 7973 is at Crewe Works for attention. Photograph by George C. Lander courtesy Rail Photoprints.

TANKS

Above **NO. 7145**

The Midland Railway used 0-6-0T locomotives mainly for shunting and local freight movements. Fowler developed S.W. Johnson's 2441 Class before Grouping by rebuilding the class with Belpaire fireboxes and this was used as a basis for the 3F introduced by the LMSR in 1924. Despite the MR influence, none of the class was built at Derby and only Horwich was involved with construction, then only contributing 15 engines. The class total of 422 was achieved by contractors, with Vulcan Foundry building the most (120), followed by William Beardmore and Hunslet Engine Co. (90 each). No. 7145 was erected by the latter company as part of the first order in February 1925. The engine is perhaps pictured slightly later in the decade as the number is on the tank side and an early version of the LMSR branding on the coal bunker. Also, in 1934 the engine was renumbered 7305.

Opposite above **NO. 16487 – LIVERPOOL EDGE HILL GOODS DEPOT**

Edge Hill, Liverpool, was the location for a station on the Liverpool & Manchester Railway when opened in 1830. The terminus was the nearby Crown Street station. Yet, this was too far from the city centre and Edge Hill later became the point where the new line to Lime Street station deviated from the original. Branches to Garston and Bootle were also subsequently connected, making Edge Hill a suitable place for a goods yard. This was built in the late 19th century by the LNWR and at the busiest periods, the yard could handle 2,000 wagons, with much of the shunting done by gravity. This image was captured at Edge Hill goods station, likely in the early 1930s, looking to the passenger station, with Fowler 3F Class 0-6-0T no. 16487 shunting wagons. The locomotive was built by the Vulcan Foundry in December 1926 and carried the original number to 1934 when becoming no. 7404.

Opposite below **NO. 7260 – SOUTH TOTTENHAM AND STAMFORD HILL STATION**

Fowler 3F Class 0-6-0T no. 7260 has a freight service at South Tottenham and Stamford Hill station, c. 1940. The line was originally a venture to connect the Great Eastern Railway at Tottenham with North West London, but these plans failed to pass Parliament and ended at Gospel Oak. In the 1870s, the Midland Railway took over as the route passed nearby and later extended eastward to Forest Gate where a junction was formed with the London, Tilbury & Southend Railway.

Above **NO. 1511 – DERBY**

Apparently fresh from a repair at Derby in the mid-1920s is no. 1511. The 0-4-0ST locomotive was one of ten forming the 1116A Class produced by the MR in the 1890s. Most left traffic in the 1920s, though one worked to 1955. No. 1511 was condemned in 1928 only to be purchased for further service at Pentrich Colliery, Derbyshire.

Opposite above **NO. 16046 – ARDROSSAN**

The Industrial Revolution spurred the development of Ardrossan as exports of goods increased and shipbuilding became established as an industry. The port was also a place for ferries to cross from Western Scotland to Belfast and the Isle of Arran. There was a network of rail lines serving the docks and these were mainly operated by the Glasgow & South Western Railway, which controlled the area between Carlisle and Glasgow. James Manson was Locomotive Superintendent between 1890 and 1911. Amongst a number of classes he produced was the 272 0-4-0T which consisted of six engines for shunting duties. No. 16046 was constructed at Kilmarnock Works in December 1908 and left traffic during 1930. The engine is paused between shunting duties at Ardrossan docks in 1926. Photograph courtesy Rail Photoprints.

Opposite below **NO. 3001 – CREWE WORKS**

Ramsbottom 4ft 0-4-0ST shunter no. 3001 takes too much water at Crewe Works during the mid-1920s. A total of 56 locomotives were erected to the design and many were inherited by the LMSR though the company soon found them superfluous and all had been condemned by the early 1930s. One working for a private firm managed to survive into the National Collection. Photograph courtesy Rail Photoprints.

CARRIAGES

Above **ROYAL SCOT FIRST-CLASS COMPARTMENT**
In 1929, the LMSR introduced a new first-class coach to diagram 1717. These had a brake compartment and four areas for passengers, seating four, with a lavatory also provided. A high standard of finish was present. Wilton carpets covered the floor and Indian Greywood was used on the walls. Mouldings and inlays were of oak and fittings were silver. The type of carriage was used in the 'Royal Scot' train.

Opposite above **ROYAL SCOT KITCHEN CAR NO. 30073**
As an experiment, the LMSR built two kitchen cars using all-electric cooking equipment in 1933. In other railway applications, the drawback of this was charging the batteries, yet the LMSR provided a diesel engine to generate the electricity. No. 30073 was sent to America with the Royal Scot locomotive and train in 1933 and is being loaded on to the boat here.

Opposite below **ROYAL SCOT THIRD-CLASS VESTIBULE COACH**
For third-class passengers, the LMSR favoured open or vestibule carriages from Grouping and into the 1930s. A large number were constructed during this period and an example used with the 'Royal Scot' train is illustrated.

Above CORONATION SCOT COCKTAIL BAR

Though the 1937 'Coronation Scot' train was modern, a new dedicated train was ordered in 1938 for the 1939 trip to America and prospective service in 1940. These were to be articulated pairs and one featured a cocktail lounge serving the first-class saloons. Two ladies are featured at the bar which has a backdrop by Nicolas Bentley who was an illustrator of distinction during the period. The theme is early rail travel in contrast to the modern high-speed and streamlined 'Coronation Scot'.

Opposite above CORONATION SCOT SET

The LMSR set a 6 hour 30 minute schedule for the 'Coronation Scot' when introduced in July 1937. The train consisted of nine carriages weighing 297 tons and were: corridor first brake, corridor first, open first, kitchen car, two open thirds, kitchen car, open third, corridor third. Seating was for 232, though places were left in the open cars for passengers from the compartments when taking a meal. These coaches were taken from stock and decorated blue with silver stripes to match the locomotive, though were internally refitted before use. The train took the time slot previously used by the 'Midday Scot' and left both north and south ends of the line at 13.30, with a scheduled arrival time of 20.00. A two-minute stop occurred at Carlisle. A surcharge of 2s 6d was in place for all travellers.

Opposite below CORONATION SCOT CLUB SALOON

The LMSR operated a relatively small number of 'club cars' for services to and around North West England. Whilst the pre-Grouping companies had made dedicated carriages, the LMSR mainly converted older stock. In the late 1930s, the decision was made to introduce one club car as part of the 'Coronation Scot' and one of two LMSR new club cars was built for the train. This was no. 823 erected at Derby in 1939 and was of standard dimensions for this era, with an interior panelled in oak. Seating was of coral pink leather armchairs. A striking contrast of décor surely matched by the equally large discrepancy with modern ideas of travel, as judged by this publicity image of the club car. Namely, drinking, smoking, reading and conversing with fellow passengers.

Above **CORONATION SCOT COCKTAIL LOUNGE**
Another view of the 'Coronation Scot' cocktail lounge. The remainder of the coach was occupied by 2½ first-class compartments and lavatory, with the other carriage an open dining saloon seating 44.

Below **CORONATION SCOT FIRST-CLASS CARRIAGE**
Three first-class compartment carriages were built for the 'Coronation Scot' in 1937 at Wolverton. No. 1069, pictured, was the first to diagram 1960.

Above and below **CORONATION SCOT FIRST-CLASS VESTIBULE COACH**

A new design of open first-class carriage was placed in production by the LMSR in 1934 to diagram 1902. First numbering 25 examples, in 1939 a further ten were built, both batches at Wolverton. With 42 seats, the coaches mainly operated as dining cars. No. 7507, illustrated, was amongst the first built in 1934 and was converted with two others for use in the 'Coronation Scot' during 1937. The interior is depicted below.

Above **FIRST-CLASS CORRIDOR BRAKE**
The initial LMSR first-class brake design was introduced in 1927 and numbered 25 examples to diagram 1654. In 1929, the second diagram, 1717, appeared from Derby consisting of six and a solitary carriage in 1932 for an accident replacement. For the diagram 1717 the brake compartment was enlarged and a bigger lavatory was provided. Seating was reduced from six to four per compartment, resulting in a capacity of 16 (down from 27). A compartment in the diagram 1717 first brake is illustrated.

Opposite above and below **CORONATION SCOT SET TO AMERICA**
As mentioned, the LMSR decided to introduce a new 'Coronation Scot' train set for 1939, particularly as the company planned to travel to America for the New York World's Fair. Though eleven carriages were to be in the running formation, seven were chosen to cross the Atlantic, with another not part of the set. These were: brake first corridor, first corridor; first corridor/cocktail lounge, first vestibule dining; kitchen, third-class vestibule dining; first-class sleeper (not part of standard formation); club car. The eleven carriages in the envisaged set consisted of: corridor first brake, corridor first; first semi-open vestibule dining car, first vestibule dining car; kitchen, third-class vestibule dining car; third semi-open vestibule dining car, corridor third; corridor third; corridor third, corridor third brake. A feature of the set was articulation (two bodies which shared a bogie in the centre) and the colour scheme was also changed from blue to red. The eight coaches left Southampton for America in January 1939, with the dining coach being lifted here above and the bogies carrying the sleeping carriage below. Three sets were scheduled to be in service for the 1940 timetable, yet the outbreak of war halted the project with some carriages completed. The order was ultimately cancelled and the existing stock dispersed.

Top FIRST-CLASS CORRIDOR BRAKE

No. 15556, renumbered 5098, is a diagram 1717 first-class brake carriage, the interior of which is seen on page 101. Interestingly, the four compartments did not share the same upholstery and different types were used in each.

Above FIRST-CLASS SEMI-OPEN COACH

Semi-open first-class carriages were introduced from Derby in 1928. These were built to diagram 1707 and numbered five examples. There were three compartments with four seats each, a lavatory and a saloon with 18 seats which could also be used for dining. The first of the five was no. 15412 which later became no. 1023 in the 1932 renumbering. The coach was preserved subsequently.

Opposite above FIRST-CLASS LOUNGE

Five first-class lounges were built to diagram 1741 in 1928. Seating was for ten and a brake compartment was also included. During the war, all were stopped and by 1950 the quintet had been converted to full brakes.

Opposite below DINING SALOON

A number of saloons were built in 1925 and these were used in general service as well as for dining. An interior is illustrated.

Above **FIRST-CLASS VESTIBULE CARRIAGE**

The interior of no. 15933 which was a first-class vestibule coach built to diagram 1707 at Derby in 1928. The type marked the use of large single windows.

Opposite above **THIRD-CLASS VESTIBULE COACH**

In the early 1930s a new version of open carriage was introduced, being 60 ft long, rather than 57 ft as previously. The new type had 50 vehicles constructed initially, split equally between two diagrams for first and third class. The latter was covered by diagram 1721 and 42 seats were provided. No. 1324 was built at Derby towards the end of the batch and was later renumbered 7711.

Opposite below **COMPOSITE CORRIDOR CARRIAGE**

The interior of a third-class compartment in a composite carriage is illustrated from the mid-1940s. At this time a large number were being constructed at Wolverton and some from Derby. The main change for the type occurred in the mid-1930s and saw the reduction in the size of the third-class compartment to 6 ft 3 in. from 6 ft 6 in. The saved space was given to enlarge the lavatory compartment. Four third-class compartments were generally provided with seating for 24.

Above left **BRAKE THIRD-CLASS COMPARTMENT**
A view of a compartment in a brake third from the mid-1930s. A large number of the type appeared in the second half of the decade to diagrams 1905, 1963 and 1968. These had four compartments with a total capacity of 24.

Above right **THIRD-CLASS OPEN CARRIAGE**
A detail of the seating used in a third-class open coach in the mid- to late 1930s.

Opposite above **THIRD-CLASS VESTIBULE CARRIAGE**
Diagram 1999 introduced in 1938 saw the seating for the third-class open-type coach reduced from 60 to 56 in order for extra space to be created. Eighty-two were constructed before the war, then following the conflict another 350 examples appeared. No. 27106 was part of this second run and built at Wolverton in 1945.

Opposite middle **THIRD-CLASS COMPARTMENT COACH**
Around Grouping, the Midland Railway had over a dozen third-class corridor carriages on order. These had eight compartments measuring under 6 ft with seating for 64 people. When these became life-expired on the LMSR, some were transferred to the Northern Counties Commission in Northern Ireland. No. 234 has been refurbished and prepared for dispatch, c. 1940.

Opposite below **THIRD-CLASS OPEN CARRIAGE**
In the mid-1930s, a number of third-class open coaches were erected to diagram 1904. These had 56 seats in two sections, 32 smoking and 24 non-smoking. Two toilets were present at either end. No. 8998 was amongst 50 ordered from the Birmingham Railway Carriage & Wagon Co.

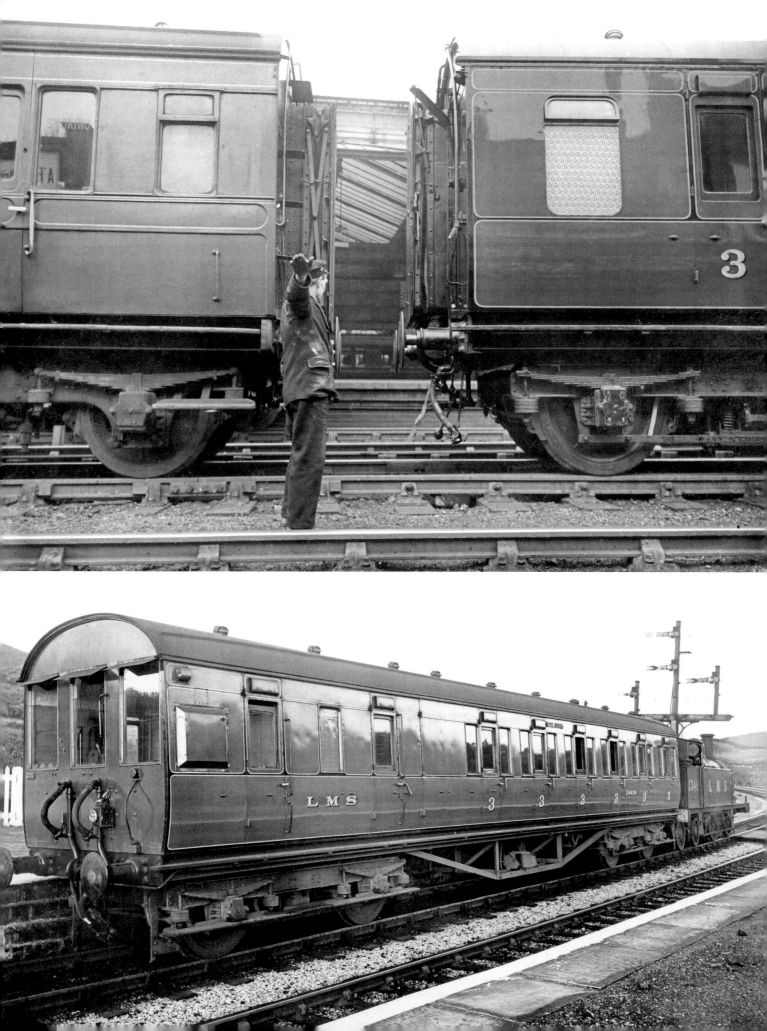

Above **THIRD-CLASS VESTIBULE COACH**
Interior of a third-class open carriage, c. 1930.

Opposite above **CARRIAGE COUPLING**
The process of coupling two carriages together is caught here, likely during the late 1930s. Though apparently both third-class vehicles, the construction is visibly different. The left coach is wooden-bodied, possessing a panelled waistline, whilst the right has a steel body. The LMSR began using steel for the exterior in the early 1930s, mainly with wooden underframes, but some built by contractors were all-steel. The use of steel also saw changes made to the livery. Crimson Lake was used for the body colour and the lining initially imitated the panelled waistline. Later, yellow lining around exterior features – windows, cant rail, etc. – broken by a black line was adopted, as displayed by the right carriage.

Opposite below **THIRD-CLASS PUSH-PULL CARRIAGE**
Instead of building dedicated stock for push-pull services, the LMSR converted existing stock. The first ones appeared in 1927 and were 54 ft-long coaches but later all were 57 ft. Third-class driving trailer no. 24404 was part of the second batch produced between 1930 and 1932. The coach is with Johnson 2228 Class 0-4-4T no. 1340 which dated from 1889. No. 24404 has a Pye Bridge destination board visible to the top centre of the coach side suggesting employment on the Ambergate-Pye Bridge branch. This connected the Midland Main Line with the Erewash Valley Line. Passenger services were withdrawn just before Nationalisation.

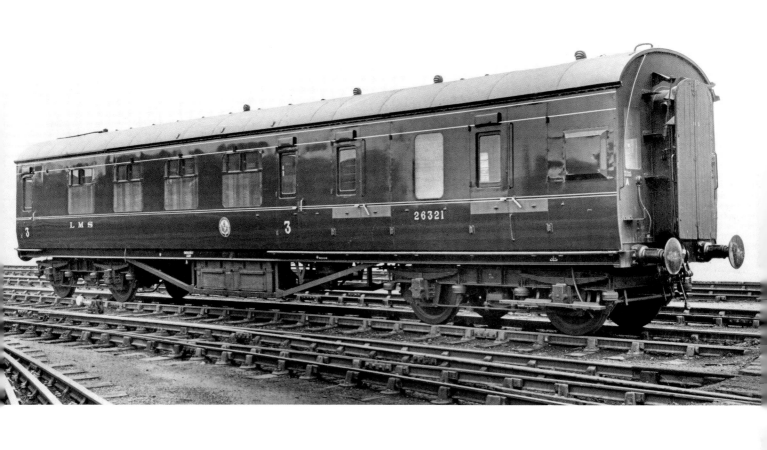

Above left and right **DINING CAR**

At Grouping, the LMSR inherited a number of combined kitchen and dining saloons. Though this might have indicated the type of services favoured by passengers, the company decided dedicated kitchen cars were necessary with open carriages serving as dining saloons. In 1930 a number of new kitchen/dining saloons were introduced, with diagram 1718 covering 12 first-class examples. The equipment present in the kitchen and pantry are shown above, with gas ranges favoured. Note the LMSR-branded kettle with 'Wolv' below, perhaps suggesting Wolverton construction. Very similar first-class kitchen/diners were built to diagram 1810 at both Wolverton and Derby at the same time, spit to six from each.

Opposite above and below **THIRD-CLASS BRAKE**

Two views of diagram 1968 third-class brake carriage no. 26321. In the early 1930s, the design of the third-class brake was changed to reduce the number of compartments from five to four and there were several detail variations covered by different diagrams. Towards the end of the decade, the interior design was modified and the lavatory moved to the end of the coach, rather than between the brake area and the passenger compartments. Diagram 1968 appeared from Derby in 1937 and 284 were built to 1939, including a batch of 56 from Wolverton. In 1945 another 50 were ordered from Derby, followed by two more lots totalling 175. No. 26321 was the first of the post-war third brakes and has the modified livery which appeared during the period. Still Crimson Lake, the lining was much simplified with a paler shade of yellow used. The number style was also slightly different as the '3' had a flat top whereas previously a curly '3' was present.

Opposite page and above **FIRST-CLASS DINING CAR**
Sixteen first-class dining carriages were built to diagram 1900 between 1933 and 1937. These had 24 seats, with six of these reserved for non-smokers. In 1947, no. 43, which was part of the last group, saw a transformation take place, with a new interior fitted. This had a mixture of seats fixed to the wall and loose seats round tables. The carriage retained 24 seats, yet the non-smoking section was removed.

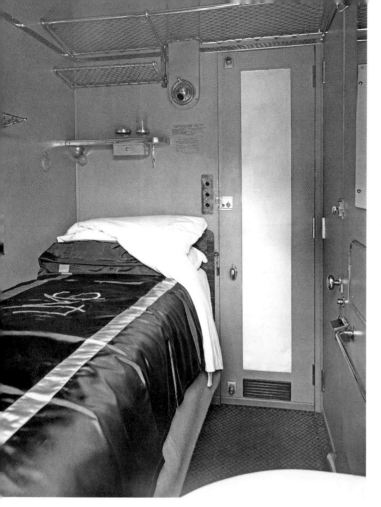 

Above left COMPOSITE SLEEPING CARRIAGE

The LMSR built a comparatively small number of composite sleeping carriages to first and third coaches. Twelve appeared in 1930-1931 from Wolverton to diagram 1781, followed by 13 to diagram 1947 in 1936 which were constructed at Derby. The latter were slightly longer at 69 ft and the arrangement of the compartments changed from the thirds flanking firsts to all thirds at one end. The first-class compartment in composite sleeper no. 713 is seen during 1936.

Above right FIRST-CLASS SLEEPER

In contrast to the later plain-styling of first-class berth, the early first-class sleepers had wooden panelling. The compartment illustrated belonged to sleeper first no. 10389 which was constructed to diagram 1739 at Wolverton in 1924. The design was slightly updated later and other first-class carriages were erected to diagram 1705 and numbered 42.

Below FIRST-CLASS SLEEPING CARRIAGE NO. 10389

An exterior view of no. 10839. Six-wheel bogies were used with the first-class and composite sleepers, whilst third-class sleepers had four-wheel bogies.

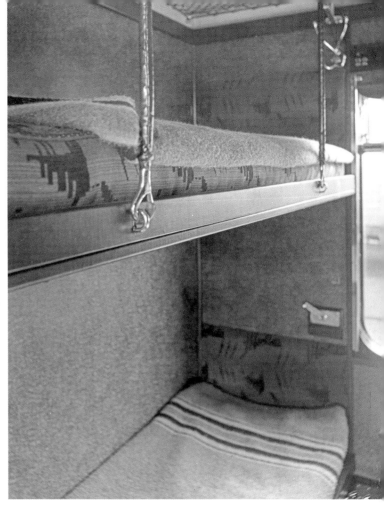

Above left **FIRST-CLASS SLEEPER BERTH**
With the wartime restrictions seeing passenger trains reduced and journey times increased, the LMSR decided to improve capacity in some first-class sleepers. This was achieved by adding a bunk bed above the original, then only in the end cabins. Around 30 carriages were converted, with diagram 1926 vehicle no. 361 illustrating the change.

Above right **THIRD-CLASS SLEEPING CARRIAGE**
When sleeping accommodation for third-class passengers was finally provided in the late 1920s, the LMSR initially produced convertible carriages which ran as normal compartment thirds in the day and the beds folded out for night use. In 1933, a small batch of 15 fixed-berth thirds were built at Derby and the interior of one is illustrated. Some of the convertibles also became fixed-berth.

Below **FIRST-CLASS SLEEPER UNDERFRAME**
The underframes for new 69 ft-long sleeper firsts were built at Derby in 1935 and shipped on for assembly at Wolverton. The distinguishing feature of these was the use of welding which replaced riveting used hitherto and provided stronger connections.

Opposite, above and below **LMSR ROYAL TRAIN**

At the turn of the century, the LNWR constructed a new Royal Train on the accession of Edward VII. These were particularly lavish 12-wheel clerestory vehicles that suited successive monarchs to the Second World War. At this time, the wooden sides were thought to be a vulnerability if the train ever came under attack, so the LMSR decided to provide three new coaches with armour plating. The image opposite illustrates the attendants' compartment in the King's Saloon of the LNWR stock, whilst above is the new King's Saloon, no. 798, and below is the supplementary sleeping/brake/power coach.

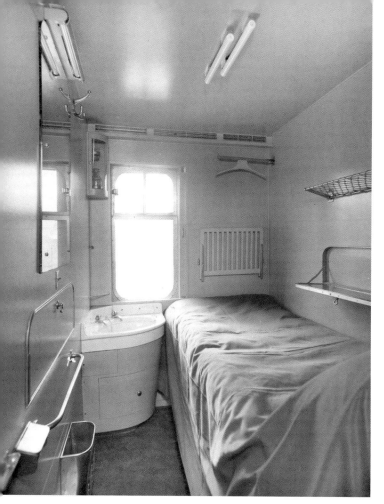

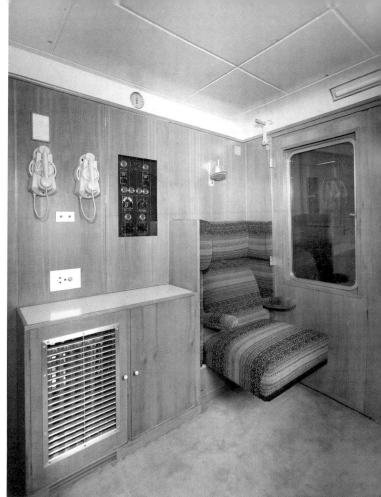

Above left **KING'S SALOON**

The King's Saloon, no. 798, was built at Wolverton to diagram 2054 in 1941. The coach was 69 ft long with two six-wheel bogies. Four main rooms were included: lounge; bedroom; bathroom; attendants' berth. These were flanked by two entrance lobbies and there was also a lavatory at one end. The attendant's berth is pictured here.

Above right **QUEEN'S SALOON**

A Queen's Saloon, no. 799, was also built at Wolverton in 1941 to diagram 2055. The layout was mirrored in relation to the King's Saloon with the same rooms. The entrance lobby, with attendant's chair and telephones, is shown above.

Below **QUEEN'S SALOON**

Both the King's and Queen's Saloons had removable armour plating, which was later permanently taken off the carriages at the end of the Second World War. The total weights were 56 tons for no. 798 and no. 799 was 57 tons. Other features were drophead buffers, Pullman gangways and buckeye couplers. The livery was Crimson Lake with the late-style lining.

Above **ROYAL MAIL CARRIAGE**

The Manchester & Liverpool Railway started the movement of mail by rail on 11th November 1830. The Railways (Conveyance of Mails) Act 1838 compelled railway companies to transport the post as part of an ordinary or special train. In the same year, the Grand Junction Railway converted a horse box, starting the Travelling Post Office. The first dedicated mail train ran on the GWR main line between Paddington and Bristol in 1855. Based on an idea from a Crewe Works Carriage and Wagon Superintendent dating from 1838, the first mail pick-up apparatus was installed in 1866 near Slough and Maidenhead. In the early 20th century nearly 130 Travelling Post Office carriages were at work in Britain. In 25 years, the LMSR erected around 50 vehicles for the transportation and sorting of mail, many of these being one-for-one replacement and designed for specific routes or duties. The first appeared from Wolverton in 1929 and the various diagrams appeared into the 1950s. No. 3275 was the first of three erected at Wolverton (as all were) in 1930 to diagram 1793. The type was mainly used for storage of mail rather than sorting and no mail pick-up apparatus is fitted to no. 3275, though one of the three was from new. No. 3275 was later renumbered 30210.

Above **CORRIDOR BRAKE**
Interior of a new corridor brake carriage from around 1929. This could be brake first no. 15556 which was built in the year as the number is partially visible on the door to the left.

Opposite above and below **ARTICULATED VESTIBULE CARRIAGE**
In the mid-1930s, there was some concern at the LMSR that the weight ratio between passengers carried and the coaching stock was too large. As a solution to this, Stanier decided to trial the use of articulation where carriage bodies shared a bogie. In 1935 an articulated triplet was created as a trial, then in 1937 a number of sets were built at Derby, being non-corridor triplet and twin vestibule sets. The underframe used and the body of a twin vestibule set under construction are pictured during early 1937.

Below **BRAKE CARRIAGE**
A large number of passenger brake coaches were ordered shortly after Grouping. These were built by outside contractors, including no. 6205, which was the product of the Birmingham Railway Carriage & Wagon Co. The carriages were of all-steel construction and had non-standard underframes. Diagram 1715 covered these coaches.

Left and below PASSENGER AMENITIES

A pair of publicity photographs taken to promote services offered by the LMSR. On the left a porter is engaged moving luggage at Leeds Wellington station in the mid-1930s. Below, pillows and rugs are offered for hire to passengers at Euston station shortly after Grouping.

Above and below **CAMPING COACHES AT HEYSHAM**

In the early 1930s, the London & North Eastern Railway developed an idea where old coaching stock was placed at several scenic locations in their area and offered as holiday destinations. This proved popular and spread to the LMSR in 1934, with 42 vehicles converted and one of the sets was placed at Heysham, south of Morecambe. Up to the Second World War, nearly 250 coaches were repurposed and spread across Britain.

WAR WORK

Above **FEMALE PORTERS**
The LMSR had a staff of around 250,000 in the late 1930s and nearly a fifth were taken by the Armed Forces during the Second World War. To fill this gap, the company held men due for retirement, re-hired those who had and accepted women for employment in a number of areas. Women were initially taken into low-ranking jobs but necessity soon saw them moving into other areas. Some 250 different railway positions were occupied by women employees, including: architects; blacksmiths; concrete workers; electricians; fitters; guards; painters; sailmakers; signalwomen; weigh-bridge attendants; etc. In total 39,000 women worked for the LMSR during the war. A group is seen moving petrol cans from a lorry to a wagon here.

Opposite page **PRIME MINISTER'S TRAIN**
For his various engagements around the country during the Second World War, Winston Churchill and his entourage were provided with a train by the LMSR. Vehicles in the formation were: brake first; two saloons; open first; dining first; sleeping carriage. To meet the Prime Minister's needs, a saloon was modified to his specifications. This train was used on both the LMSR's lines and those of the other railway companies. The lounge and conference room of the train are seen here.

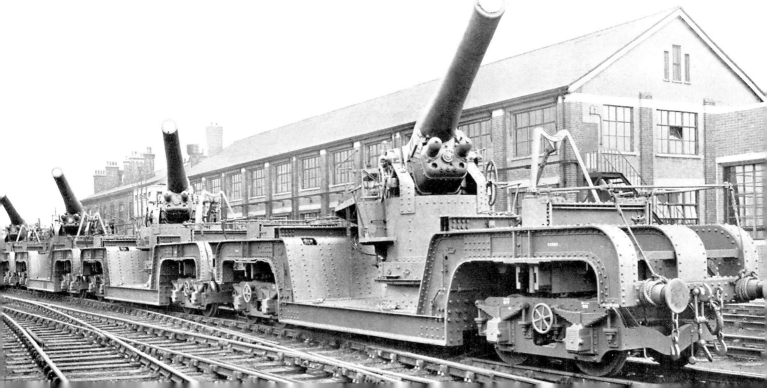

Opposite and above WAR PRODUCTION

The LMSR was placed under Government control at the start of the Second World War, along with the other railway companies. They were operated under the Railway Executive Committee which was overseen by the Minister for War Transport. At the start of the conflict, the company played a key role in the evacuation of children and 1,450 trains ran, carrying approx. 500,000 people. Then came the preparations for war, which included providing air-raid warnings to passengers and staff, keeping traffic moving where possible, protecting vital places, such as signal boxes, stations, sheds, etc., preparing for repairs and enforcing blackout conditions. Troop movements were also numerous and 164 military trains ran under the LMSR following the outbreak of war. The company was soon called on to bring soldiers back from the Dunkirk evacuation and 44 of the 186 trains created for the task were LMSR-donated. The LMSR held one of the largest engineering operations in the world which employed nearly 25,000 across dozens of workshops. Nearly 5,000 Government orders for munitions, guns, tanks, aeroplanes, etc., were completed to 1945. At the height of the conflict 32% of the workforce was engaged in war production whilst having to continue to service locomotives, carriages and wagons. At Derby, the shops produced sections of aircraft, as well as repairing damaged parts. Around 4,000 wings were built for various designs. The works also completed 17- and 25-pound guns and several types of tanks: A13 Cruisers; Centaurs; Covenanters; Matildas.

ROAD VEHICLES

Above **HORSE-DRAWN EXPRESS PARCELS VAN**

The Midland Railway's 2¼-ton covered parcels van was chosen to be a standard design for the LMSR shortly after Grouping. The company offered a nationwide service conveying parcels between stations, but also selected independent traders which increased availability. This MR vehicle is seen in new LMSR Crimson Lake livery with lining and the frame on the canvas cover could be used for advertisements. Some vans later had much of the canvas given over to publicity materials which no doubt generated a healthy income.

Opposite above **FLAT DRAY**

A Type 87 3¼-ton flat dray is moving a model of new Cunard-White Star liner *Queen Mary*. This had been constructed at Northampton, possibly by Bassett-Lowke, for Cunard-White Star's offices and is on the way there here. The model was 24-ft long and weighed 50 cwt.

Opposite below **FLAT DRAY AND OPEN WAGON**

In the mid-1920s, containerised transport of goods was promoted by the LMSR to reduce handling between shipping points. Several vehicles were developed, including open wagons which were chained to flat wagons then lifted on to drays for final delivery. Initially wood, a subsequent development was metal wagons and one is pictured. Loaded on a flat dray, delivery of tiles is carried out at Roberts Aldard & Co. Ltd.

Above **OPEN VAN**

A 5-ton open van has been loaded at an unidentified goods station. The type was particularly suited to urban environments owing to the high seat position and utilised a pair of horses. These were often matched together so the work could be shared equally. At Grouping, the LMSR had over 9,000 horses and this number slightly increased before declining as motor vehicles took a greater share of the traffic. Just over 6,000 were still employed at Nationalisation. The horses were bought by the LMSR at five years old and worked for around another five. The horses' day lasted approx. 14 hours, with three feeds and watering occurring during that period. The LMSR was involved in producing the provender (hay, straw and grain) for the animals and this amounted to 36,000 tons annually. Several large horse hospitals were provided and the welfare of the horses was a particular consideration. Staff were encouraged to take an interest and parades took place often.

Opposite above **AEC BUS**

A small number of omnibuses were operated by the LNWR at Grouping, yet the LMSR soon found that road competition for local services was a force to be reckoned with. The company was restricted as a new Act of Parliament was needed to offer omnibus services. Though an initial attempt failed in 1924, a second bill passed in 1928 and this gave the railways free rein to operate their own companies, or enter partnership with existing or prospective firms to provide road-going services. In the next three years just over £100,000 was invested in omnibuses and associated companies. A problem encountered was that the established concerns were well positioned to exploit the LMSR's interest in the industry leading to inflation of prices and forecasts. The result was the company had to be more cautious as the 1930s progressed, as well as the economic downturn occurring. Most omnibuses ordered by the LMSR were built in 1929, with this example appearing in June. Carrying registration UR3766, the bus had an AEC Reliance chassis with a body supplied by Cravens Ltd and went to work in Sheffield.

Opposite below **ALBION BUS**

An interesting feature of this Albion vehicle is the sliding canvas roof.

BUSES

Above **ROAD-RAIL BUS**
A novel project instigated by the LMSR in the late 1920s was a bus that was capable of switching between the road and railway. A chassis was obtained from Karrier Motors Ltd and a body was fitted to this at Cravens Ltd. Starting work in November 1930, the road-rail bus was used on the Stratford-upon-Avon & Midland Junction Railway line which connected the Midland Railway's route to Gloucester and the Northampton branch. The road-rail bus was only in use for around a year before withdrawn.

Below **OMNIBUS**
The LMSR ordered over 50 omnibuses and an unidentified type is pictured below. Note the roof is another convertible example.

LORRIES

Above **KARRIER LORRY**
This Karrier-supplied chassis has a Midland Railway-style cab.

Below **AEC CONTAINER LORRY**
Two containers advertising the LMSR's furniture removal service are with an AEC lorry and trailer.

Above **MORRIS COMMERCIAL LORRY**
Initially starting with a bicycle business, William Morris diversified into motor vehicles during 1912 and soon built a successful company. In the mid-1920s, he bought the assets of a failed axle and gearbox manufacturer and used this as a springboard for establishing an arm for commercial lorry construction. These ranged from under a ton capacity to five tons. An early example is depicted here at Llandudno grain shed showing the transfer of grain from railway van to motor lorry.

Opposite above and below **SCAMMELL 25-TON LORRY**
Like William Morris, George Scammell was involved with another industry and expanded into motor vehicles. He was a coachbuilder before starting Scammell Lorries Ltd in 1922. Scammell initially specialised in articulated lorries and a 25-ton design features here with a load being moved from Hendon to West India Docks in 1930. The load is a saturator made by the Chemical Engineering Co. Ltd, weighing 12 tons 13 cwt and measuring 12 ft x 12 ft x 12 ft. A permanent way crane has been engaged to move the load from the railway to the Scammell.

Above **CONTAINER LOADER**

With the introduction of container traffic in the late 1920s, cranes were a distinct necessity for lifting them between the rail and road. Walker Brothers, Wigan, had entered the commercial vehicle market in the early 1920s and was able to supply the LMSR. The crane is in action moving a BX-type container.

Below **SCAMMELL 25-TON LORRY**

Another view of the Scammell 25-ton lorry. The maximum speed of the cab is 12 mph, whilst the trailer is 4 mph – note the chain drive to the rear wheels.

Above CONTAINER CRANE

The Walker travelling crane was mounted on a six-wheel lorry chassis and had solid wheels. A second set of normal tyres were also provided for movement on roads. The cranes were generally confined to goods yards, where fixed cranes were also employed. Whilst the crane seen opposite is numbered 42X, the example above is 36X and is pictured in early 1930.

Above **FURNITURE REMOVALS**

The introduction of containerised goods movement in the late 1920s, also lent itself to furniture removals. Dedicated containers were developed for the traffic.

Opposite **GUY GOODS LORRIES**

As with buses, the LMSR bought chassis and made bodies for these. This was done at Derby initially, before being transferred to Wolverton. The company also bought complete vehicles which came from all the well-known manufacturers of the period. A fleet of ten Guy Motors flatbed lorries are at an unidentified goods facility here, likely in the mid- to late 1930s. Guy Motors was founded in 1914 and subsequently won several contracts from the Government during the First World War. In the inter-war period, the company branched into motor car manufacture, lorries and buses.

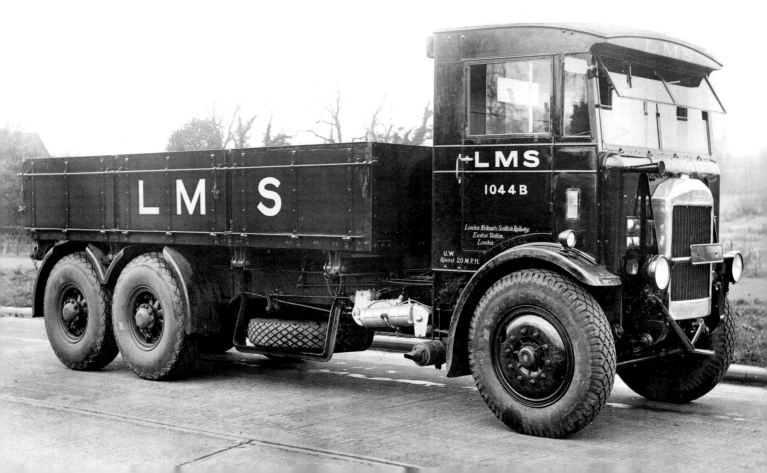

Above **KARRIER LORRY**

Unloading at Abergele & Pensarn station c. 1934 is a Karrier lorry, registration UR990. Located just west of Bangor, the station opened with the Chester & Holyhead Railway in 1848. In the *Railway Clearing House* of 1938, Abergele & Pensarn station was noted with all facilities: goods; parcels; furniture vans, motor cars, etc.; livestock; horseboxes. The capacity of the fixed crane at the station was 5 tons.

Opposite above **LIVESTOCK LORRY**

This is possibly a Fordson 'A' truck which has been fitted with a body for transporting livestock, in this instance pigs. The LMSR created some of these with the rear section removable and convertible for other purposes. The ramps allowing access folded for movement and the guide rails were carried on the side of the body.

Opposite below **DENNIS LORRY**

Dennis Brothers began as a manufacturer of bicycles before founding an automobile business at the start of the 20th century. Just before the First World War, the company focused on lorries as the brothers felt this area was underrepresented. Following the conflict, the market was saturated with surplus war vehicles so the focus switched to buses, fire engines and dustbin lorries. Dennis remained involved in lorry construction and was obliged to build them for the Ministry of Supply between 1939-1945. A Dennis tipper lorry – possibly dating from the mid-1930s – is pictured. The vehicle has a 12-ton capacity.

Above **MORRIS COMMERCIAL LORRIES**
A pair of six-wheel Morris Commercial vehicles have been recorded loaded with mill machinery for Whalley Bank Mills, Blackburn. The lorries appear to be fitted with a Wolverton-designed cab.

Opposite above **LORRY ON WEIGHBRIDGE AT ST PANCRAS STATION**
Industrial machinery is loaded on a lorry which sits on the weighbridge at St Pancras station in the early 1930s. This served two purposes: to ensure load was in limit of lorry; calculate carriage fees.

Opposite below **ALBION 5-TON LORRY**
Concrete blocks are loaded on to an Albion 5-ton lorry during the early 1930s.

Above **CONTAINER**
Eggs are loaded from the Gloucestershire Marketing Society Limited's Poultry Plucking Station & Stores into an LMSR container during the mid-1930s.

Opposite above **SCAMMELL LORRY**
In the *LMS Magazine* of October 1928, the company stated: 'The Container system…has not been based on the economics of goods-station operation, but as a commercial facility of great value to traders, while at the same time enabling the railway companies to meet certain forms of road competition at least on equal terms.' The LMSR had paid particular attention to the size of the containers and tried to keep their weight to a minimum. At the time of the article around 800 were in service. The lowest load carried was one ton and the piece claimed that costs of packaging for the supplier was reduced by using the container against standard methods. A Type B container is moved from rail to waiting Scammell lorry, c. 1935. The crane appears to be a Ransome & Rapier example which was fixed to the chassis rather than swivel for the Walker type.

Opposite below **LORRY**
A six-wheel, flatbed lorry is seen in the late 1930s.

Above INSULATED CONTAINER

In the 1930s, over half of British meat consumption was met by animals reared abroad – from the Empire, Denmark (pigs) and America – owing to favourable import tariffs. These also allowed much of the nation's sugar, flour and cheese to be shipped into the country. On arrival, suitable methods of transport were necessary and an insulated container was developed – for both meat and fish – to reduce intermediate handling. This insulated container is making a delivery to Smithfield Market in the late 1930s.

Opposite above INSULATED ROAD-RAIL TANKER

For bulk liquid movement, the LMSR developed the road-rail tanker. This was loaded on to a railway flat wagon and secured using chains. At the destination, the tanker was paired with a Scammell Mechanical Horse for transport to the destination. Variants on this saw another one or two axles provided for a trailer-type connection rather than the articulated kind in use here.

Opposite below DENNIS LORRY

A Dennis 6-ton articulated flatbed lorry is seen during the late 1930s.

Above **SCAMMELL SIX-TON MECHANICAL HORSE**
As mentioned, women answered the call for help as men left the railways during the war. They were used in all facets of operations and one is behind the wheel of a Scammell 6-ton Mechanical Horse apparently loaded with timber here in 1941.

Opposite above **LEYLAND LORRY**
Leyland Motors started just before the turn of the century producing steam-powered vehicles. In the early 1900s, the company was building all types of motor vehicles using petrol and diesel engines. In the late 1920s, Leyland introduced the 'Hippo' model with a six-cylinder L6 diesel engine and this ran with a number of variations to the end of the company in the late 1960s. An eight-axle flatbed 'Hippo' is being loaded with what appears to be metal bars using a magnetised crane attachment during the late 1930s.

Opposite below **TRAVELLING CRANE**
Though well known for producing agricultural equipment, International Harvester also diversified into motor vehicles. One of the company's truck chassis has been modified to carry a crane unit by Bay City. The image dates from the 1940s.

VANS

Above **EXPRESS PARCELS VANS**
The LMSR had stipulations for the design of the express parcels vans. These were for a compact, rigid vehicle with low cab allowing ease of descending to the ground. The Dennis Ace met these specifications and a number are pictured in an unidentified yard. The LMSR later went further by requiring the engine to be behind the front axle for better servicing.

Opposite above **TRAVELLING CRANE**
A post-war travelling crane built by Walker Brothers, Wigan, poses here with crew.

Opposite below **DENNIS TRUCK**
With petrol in short supply during the Second World War, other fuels were used. 'Town Gas', which was a by-product of the coking process, found favour for a time, yet this was not compressible and had to be carried in a large bag, usually fitted to the roof. Natural gas was also noted in use in France during the war and this could be the application here, though no details have come to light. This Dennis lorry is recorded as being fitted with Mk II gas producers in the early 1940s.

Above **JOINT PARCELS VAN**

At Grouping, the LMSR became joint operators of the ex-Midland & Great Northern Joint Railway which extended into East Anglia from Peterborough with the London & North Eastern Railway. This was the largest joint venture in Britain at the time with over 180 route miles of track. In the spirit of partnership, the road vehicles operated under both parties were branded LMS & LNE, with one small parcels van so treated. The smart-looking cartage man is wearing a standard uniform of black suit with cap. Other items issued for cold weather included overcoat and canvas raincoat.

Opposite above **DENNIS FOUR-TON VAN**

A Dennis 4-ton van is seen in 1937. The vehicle had been recently painted, with the date on the front wheel arch noting 17th August. Like locomotives, motor vehicles had two liveries depending on their roles. Parcels vans were given Crimson Lake livery with modest yellow lining. Letters on the top panel were in cream, whilst the company branding below was in yellow shaded by dark red.

Opposite below **ALBION FIVE-TON LORRY**

This Albion 5-ton lorry was modified to possess a moving floor in the late 1930s.

RAILWAY STATIONS

Above BROOM JUNCTION STATION

Connecting the Northamptonshire iron ore mines to the steel mills in South Wales was the chief aim for the Northampton & Banbury Junction Railway when originally promoted in the late 1840s. Yet, financial backers did not share the company's enthusiasm and the first section was not completed until the mid-1860s and the line finally reached Banbury in 1872. A branch from this to Stratford-upon-Avon was built at the same time and opened in the early 1870s. This line proved quite unprofitable and closed to passengers for ten years, 1875-1885. In this time the operating company – East & West Junction Railway – still saw the value in freight traffic and extended westward from Stratford-upon-Avon to Broom where the Evesham branch between Barnt Green and Ashchurch passed through. At the other end of the route, an extension was made from Towcester to Roade and Olney, meeting the LNWR and MR in the process. When the line was complete a new company was formed – Stratford-upon-Avon & Midland Junction Railway. This became part of the LMSR at Grouping. Broom Junction station opened in June 1879 for exchange and 1880 for local passengers. This service was lost in 1949 and complete closure occurred in the early 1960s.

Opposite above CALLANDER STATION

A short line from Dunblane to Callander opened in 1858. This was extended to Oban in the late 1860s and completed in 1870, with a new station built at Callander. Closure occurred in 1965.

Opposite below BRADFORD FORSTER SQUARE STATION

Two views of Bradford Forster Square station, c. 1930. This was the third station to stand on the site following the original built by the Leeds & Bradford Railway and a second erected by the Midland Railway in the mid-1850s. The latter company constructed the third station during 1890 and this stood for 100 years when a new facility was created.

FORSTER SQUARE   FORSTER SQUARE

Above **EAST HAM STATION**

The London, Tilbury & Southend Railway opened East Ham station in 1858 as the company laid a more convenient line from Bow to Barking. London & Blackwall Railway and Eastern Counties Railway lines had been in use hitherto. At the turn of the century, the District Railway reached East Ham and at this time a new station was provided. The frontage is pictured festooned in advertisements for LMSR services. All of these are day excursions, with the destinations being: Malo les Baines, Dunkirk; Dunoon, Argyll and Bute; Isle of Man; 'Bracing' Blackpool. Regular services to Southend are also advertised.

Opposite above **BURY BOLTON STREET STATION**

In September 1846, the East Lancashire Railway opened their line from Clifton (where a connection was made to the Manchester & Bolton Railway) to Rawtenstall via Bury. At the end of the 1850s, the ELR became part of the Lancashire & Yorkshire Railway which also had another station in Bury. This had been built by the Liverpool & Bury Railway in 1848 and to distinguish between the two the L&YR renamed both in 1866. The ELR facility became Bury Bolton Street and the L&BR Bury Market Place, though this later became Bury Knowsley Street. A new station was built at Bolton Street in the 1880s and was also the location for the L&YR's headquarters. The station frontage is seen around Grouping.

Opposite below **CHESTERFIELD STATION**

Chesterfield was first served by rail thanks to the North Midland Railway which established a station in 1840 on the opening of the Derby to Leeds line. At this time, the company bypassed Sheffield owing to adverse gradients, though the MR rectified this oversight when a loop was laid in 1870. Chesterfield was provided with a new station and the buildings were in use until 1963. The platforms are viewed here in the 1920s.

Above **FARNWORTH & BOLD STATION**

Though the St Helens & Runcorn Gap Railway was open from 1833, the line was built to serve mineral interests and delivered coal to the River Mersey at Widnes. In the late 1840s, the route was improved greatly and passenger trains were offered from 1852. Farnworth station was built at this time just to the north east of Widnes. The line was absorbed by the LNWR in 1864. The company had to rename the station Farnworth & Bold following the opening of the Cheshire Lines Committee station nearby. Under the LMSR around a dozen passenger trains were offered and one has stopped to collect travellers. During the war the number of trains was cut in half and this remained past Nationalisation to closure for passenger traffic in 1951.

Opposite above and below **EUSTON STATION**

The London & Birmingham Railway was authorised in 1833, yet the scheme had been active for a decade. At the start of the 1830s, the project was well subscribed but meeting much opposition from landowners. This was true for the length of the line and particularly so at the London end where the terminus was prevented from penetrating past the New Road – later Euston Road – to the more advantageous central area. Euston station was designed by Philip Hardwick with a train shed by Charles Fox and opening occurred for the first section northward in July 1837, followed by the complete route to Birmingham on 17th September 1838. At the end of the decade, Hardwick had completed two hotels either side of Euston Grove which ran from Euston Road. These were the first accommodation buildings built for railway passengers in London. Hardwick's son Philip Charles Hardwick enlarged the station in the late 1840s and this included the addition of the Great Hall. The two hotels, which served each class of passenger, were connected by a frontage building in 1881. This is presented opposite above in the 1920s, whilst platform seven appears opposite below. The LMSR planned to completely remodel the site in the mid-1930s using Government grants, yet this was halted by the war. British Railways followed through with a reconstruction for the West Coast Electrification and this was completed in 1968.

Above **LEIGH-ON-SEA STATION**

The new Leigh-on-Sea station is seen shortly after opening on 1st January 1934. This replaced the London Tilbury & Southend Railway's facility dating from July 1855 and was slightly further west. The first station was originally named Leigh, but a change to the present title was made in October 1904.

Opposite above **KINGS LANGLEY STATION**

The London & Birmingham's first section ran from Euston to Boxmoor, later known as Hemel Hempstead when opened in July 1837. Located just to the south, Kings Langley was not provided with a station at this time, but had to wait two years for a facility to be erected after pressure from a local businessman. On 1st October 1909, the name was modified to Kings Langley & Abbotts Langley station, though this does not appear on the station sign visible to the left. A reversion to the original was made in 1974.

Opposite below **ILKESTON TOWN STATION**

To relieve pressure on the Midland Main Line and encourage growth in the Nottinghamshire coalfield, the Midland Railway built the Erewash Valley Line from Long Eaton to Clay Cross over two sections – 1847 to Codnor Park and 1862 to Clay Cross. The first part passed just to the east of Ilkeston and the MR built a short branch there, also in 1847. For the next 23 years, this line was neglected by the company and closure took place in 1870. Prompted by the MR's dominance in the area, the Great Northern Railway built competing lines and reached Ilkeston on the way to Derby and Burton-on-Trent. This Ilkeston North station resulted in the reopening of the MR's Ilkeston as Ilkeston Town in July 1879. Shortly before Nationalisation, the LMSR closed the station owing to the ongoing problems caused by the harsh winter of 1946/1947. The facility officially ended passenger services in 1950 and goods traffic remained to 1960, with the line later lifted.

JUDGES LTD

Above LOUGHBOROUGH STATION

The Midland Counties Railway connected the London & Birmingham Railway at Rugby to Nottingham and Derby. This ran via Leicester and Loughborough and opened throughout on 1st July 1840. Loughborough station accepted traffic shortly before this on 5th May. These buildings were later replaced in 1872 and remain in use today with Grade II-listed status. Two other stations later served Loughborough. The Great Central's Loughborough Central and the LNWR opened Loughborough Derby Road. As a result, at Grouping Loughborough station became Loughborough Town briefly before taking the name Loughborough Midland. This lasted to 1970 when reverted to the original.

Opposite above MANCHESTER CENTRAL STATION

Much of industrial Lancashire was dominated by the LNWR. To break this hold, the Manchester, Sheffield & Lincolnshire Railway joined forces with the Great Northern Railway and formed the Cheshire Lines Committee. Active from the 1860s, the CLC built and acquired several lines to the early 20th century. The company's route ran to the south of Manchester, from there to Liverpool, northward to Southport, south-westward to Chester and a connection was made to the Ellesmere Port and Birkenhead line. The hub of operations in Manchester was Central station which opened in a temporary capacity from July 1877. A permanent building was ready on 1st July 1880 and was designed by Sir John Fowler with a single 210-ft-span roof that had a length of 550 ft. In 1963, the structure was awarded Grade II-listed status. The Midland Railway joined the main two companies in the enterprise during the early 1860s and this gave the LMSR a place on the Committee at Grouping, though the company remained independent until Nationalisation. Manchester Central station closed on 5th May 1969.

Opposite below
LLANFAIRPWLLGWYNGYLLGOGERYCHWYRNDROBWLLLLANTYSILIOGOGOGOCH STATION

On the line from Crewe to Holyhead, Llanfair station was opened in 1848. At this time, passengers had to transfer to a ferry for the crossing of the Menai Strait as the Britannia Bridge was not completed until 1850. Towards the end of the 19th century, there was an attempt by locals to promote the village as a tourist attraction and to do this devised the gimmick of a long name. The LMSR has joined in with the scheme by displaying the name – Llanfairpwllgwyngyllgogerychwyrndrobwllllantysiliogogogoch – prominently on a sign, though the official name remained Llanfair to closure in February 1966. When the Britannia Bridge caught fire in May 1970, the station was reopened as Llanfair PG which lasted for two years. In 1973, the facility was again in use, but with the name altered to Llanfairpwll.

L. M. S. Station Methley

Above PENRITH STATION

In the mid-1830s, thoughts of railway promoters had already turned to completing a connection from the North West to Scotland and Glasgow. Routes were surveyed and a Royal Commission also reported on the best way over the difficult ground. The Lancaster & Carlisle Railway was authorised first in 1844 before the Caledonian Railway was given the go-ahead to finish the route which connected England and Scotland in 1845. The L&CR had a path running from Lancaster to Oxenholme, Tebay, Shap, Penrith to Carlisle. Construction was relatively swift and the whole route was operational by the end of 1846. Penrith station came into use at this time and was designed by Sir William Tite, who was involved in other stations on the route, as well as others across the country. Penrith station also later served trains from the Stainmore Line and a branch to Keswick and Workington. The station was listed in 1983.

Opposite above MANCHESTER LONDON ROAD STATION

The Manchester & Birmingham Railway's first section from Manchester to Stockport was ready in 1840 and the northern terminus was at London Road. Initially, a temporary structure was used before a dedicated building was erected in 1842. The Sheffield, Ashton-under-Lyne and Manchester Railway also ran into the station at this time and continued to do so even as space became increasingly scarce. A major rebuild was undertaken in the early 1860s and this included a new train shed, passenger facilities and station frontage. Further additions were made to the site in the early 1880s. Manchester London Road remained in joint use through to Nationalisation and 1958 the two sides were joined as one. From 1960, Manchester London Road became known as Manchester Piccadilly and in 1966 a reconstruction was completed which saw some of the buildings cleared whilst retaining some of the train shed. Evening commuters are pictured walking towards the station c. 1930.

Opposite below METHLEY STATION

The North Midland Railway approached Leeds from the south east and passed the village of Methley. A station was opened there in 1841, at which time several other new stations were added to the route. Methley later became a small hub of lines as the Lancashire & Yorkshire and Great Northern Joint line from Pontefract and Knottingley joined the NMR. The two companies also joined with the North Eastern Railway to head westward and link with the Wakefield-Leeds route. The NER also connected to the NMR at Methley. Two other stations later served Methley and the original became Methley North in 1950, though this was only in use for seven years as closure took place in 1957.

Above ST BEES STATION

The Whitehaven & Furness Railway was promoted to connect the town of Whitehaven with the Furness Railway at Broughton-in-Furness. This scheme came to fruition in the late 1840s, with St Bees station open from 19th July 1849. The station buildings, seen right, are slightly later additions from 1860. At the platform is a Furness Railway D. Rutherford 115 Class 4-6-4T, no. 115. This was one of five built in 1920-1921 by Kitson & Co. for express passenger services from Carnforth to Whitehaven. The Whitehaven & Furness Railway joined with the Furness Railway in 1865 and the latter managed to remain independent to Grouping. The 115 Class did not have similar longevity and worked for just 15-20 years before scrapped by the LMSR.

Opposite above PLEAN STATION

The Scottish Central Railway branched northward from the Edinburgh & Glasgow line to reach Stirling and Perth. This route was completed in the late 1840s and in the mid-1860s the company was taken over by the Caledonian Railway. Between Larbert and Stirling, the village of Plean was passed a short distance to the east. The CR provided a station there in 1904 and this was in use to June 1956.

Opposite below POPLAR (EAST INDIA ROAD) STATION

The London & Birmingham Railway desired a connection with the docks in East London. The East & West India Docks & Birmingham Junction Railway – later North London Railway – achieved this aim in 1846, linking Islington with Bow and the London & Blackwall Railway. Extensions soon occurred at the western end, as well as the eastern in the early 1850s as a line from Bow to the docks was laid. This was freight-only until 1866 when Poplar (East India Road) station opened to the design of Thomas Matthews. His frontage is well-hidden by advertisements in this image dating c. 1930. The station was the victim of enemy action during the London Blitz, but remained operational until 1944 when completely destroyed. Poplar was not rebuilt but a new station was later provided as part of the Docklands Light Railway.

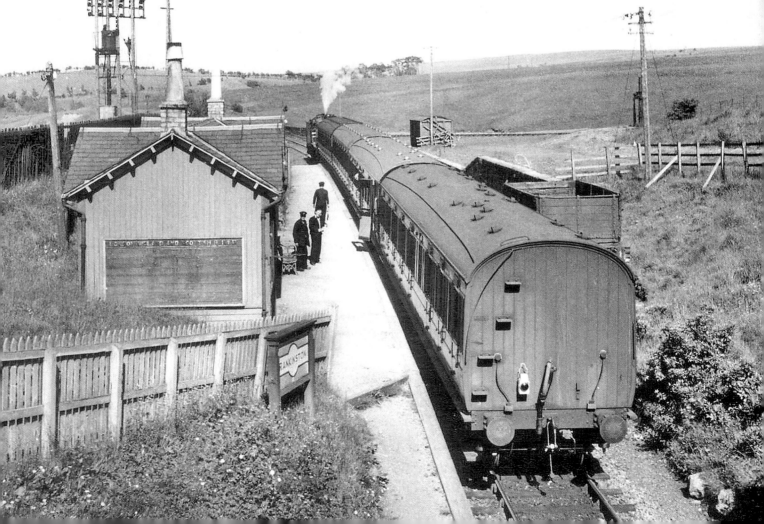

Above **STEETON STATION**
Just north of Keighley at Steeton station (on the line between Bradford and Skipton), Stanier Jubilee Class 4-6-0 no. 5581 *Bihar and Orissa* has experienced a mishap resulting in a derailment on 11th October 1943. The engine was returned to traffic and had a service life to August 1966.

Opposite above **ST PANCRAS STATION**
The Midland Railway had a dominant position in the Midlands when formed in the mid-1840s and had access to the North as well as the South West later. Yet, the company had to rely on the London & Birmingham Railway (later LNWR) for access to the Capital. Whilst beneficial to both parties at the start, ambitions outweighed these and the MR was obliged to find a new route to London. This arrived in the form of the Great Northern main line to York, which the MR joined at Hitchin in 1857 after building a connection. In the early 1860s, the MR took the bold step of creating an extension to reach London, leaving Bedford and heading southward paralleling the GNR and LNWR main lines to nestle between the two at St Pancras. The task was completed in late 1868 with the opening of St Pancras station which was designed by W.H. Barlow. He had to efficiently use the space allocated and as the running lines passed over the Regent's Canal, the station approaches were high enough to sit atop warehousing, mainly for beer from Burton-upon-Trent. Further, to reduce structural components in the goods space, Barlow chose to build a single-span roof 245 ft wide which cost around £60,000 to complete. In all, the MR's London Extension cost £9,000,000.

Opposite below **RANKINSTON STATION**
The Glasgow & South Western Railway operated much of the rail infrastructure in Ayrshire. The company laid a route from Ayr to Mauchline in 1870 and this developed with a branch southward via Ochiltree to Cronberry, then a short section connected with the Ayr and Dalmellington branch at Holehouse. Rankinston station was on this latter part and served passengers from 1st January 1884 to 3rd April 1950.

Above **WEMYSS BAY STATION**

Many vessels were restricted from navigating the River Clyde during the early to mid-19th century. As a result, unloading of goods was carried out at Greenock and a railway was promoted for this traffic. The Glasgow, Paisley & Greenock Railway opened in 1841 and was later absorbed by the Caledonian Railway. In the early 1860s, the Isle of Bute was popular with Glaswegians as a holiday destination and a line to Wemyss for these passengers was built and ready on 15th May 1865. The Wemyss Bay Railway, which joined the Greenock line near Port Glasgow, was independent to the early 1890s when also taken over by the CR. The company rebuilt Wemyss Bay station in 1903. The architect was James Miller and his design has been praised greatly over the years, resulting in listed status. The interior of the booking hall is presented and features heavy floral decorations.

Opposite above **SWANSEA ST THOMAS STATION**

The Swansea Vale Railway started as a wagonway to deliver coal to Swansea docks for transport to the West Country for copper smelting. In the 1840s the line became a railway but remained freight-only to 1860 when approved for passenger traffic. Swansea St Thomas station opened at this time as Swansea with St Thomas added several years later. The company came into the sights of the Midland Railway around this time and after negotiations with several companies, the MR was able to run from Hereford into South Wales. The SVR was taken over outright in 1876. After Grouping, the ex-MR route remained important for mineral traffic but the passenger service dwindled. Closure occurred shortly after Nationalisation as a result.

Opposite below **WOLVERHAMPTON (HIGH LEVEL) STATION**

When the Grand Junction Railway opened in 1837, the line skirted the eastern side of Wolverhampton. A station was provided, but sat around a mile away from the centre. The Birmingham, Wolverhampton & Stour Valley railway opened in the early 1850s and provided a more convenient station at Wolverhampton. The company was controlled by the LNWR which was able to reroute traffic to the new station. In the mid-1850s the Oxford, Worcester & Wolverhampton Railway opened and their station was sited on the eastern side of the LNWR facility. This new station was known as Low Level and the older subsequently became High Level. Both are advertised on the frontage of High Level station, c. 1930. Low Level was closed in 1972 and High Level was completely rebuilt in the 1960s. The station has recently seen another reconstruction take place.

STANFORD STATION v2266 V.W.L.

Above YELVERTOFT & STANFORD PARK STATION

The LNWR promoted a line from Rugby to Stamford via Market Harborough in the mid-1840s. Construction was completed in stages between 1850 and 1851. Yelvertoft & Stanford Park station was built with the first section to Market Harborough and opened on 1st May 1850. The station first appeared in the timetable as Stanford Hall in the following year for the nearby stately home. In 1870 this changed to Yelvertoft, then a decade later Yelvertoft & Stanford Hall was used, though the local landowner requested a further alteration to Yelvertoft & Stanford Park. The line was later cut as part of the Beeching Report and closure occurred on 6th June 1966.

Opposite CREWE STATION

A railway porter changes the midday departures at Crewe station during the mid-1930s. Crewe was the hub for a number of lines in the area, though might not have been if other places nearby had accepted the overtures of the Grand Junction Railway in the 1830s. On 4th July 1837, the company's line from Birmingham to Warrington was ready, with Crewe serving passengers from that time. Three years later the Chester & Crewe Railway made a connection, as did the Manchester & Birmingham and in the mid-1840s a line from Shrewsbury opened. The North Staffordshire Railway from Stoke began operations from 1848, whilst during the 1860s routes to Market Drayton and Wellington, in addition to Oswestry saw trains running. The station was adapted to this increased load in the mid-1860s and again at the turn of the century when nearly £2 million was invested in the station and environs. The LMSR improved the signalling at Crewe in the late 1930s with new boxes and equipment.

Above LMSR PORTERS
A pair of porters are busy loading parcels in the Lancashire area during the 1930s. Photograph by Sydney Garbutt courtesy Rail Photoprints.

Opposite above left STATION ANNOUNCER
With a Blackpool North-headed timetable, a station announcer informs passengers of arrivals/departures using a Tannoy-branded microphone during the late 1930s. Tannoy had been established in the 1920s and quickly developed a reputation for high-quality audio equipment, with the railways an obvious market.

Opposite above right STATION STAFF
Keeping stations clean and pleasant for passengers was no doubt a priority for all railway companies owing to the negative impressions this could cause in competitive markets. A young lad has been engaged with shovel and broom here, perhaps collecting discarded chocolate wrappers or matches and cigarette ends, with two of these available from the primitive vending machines on the right.

Opposite below left LAMP CLEANER
A row of railway lamps are to be cleaned at Bletchley station in the mid-1930s.

Opposite below right ADVERTISEMENT
Sunday excursion services to the North West and Blackpool feature on this advertisement.